This book has been written for children. Some inform
deliberately simplified to make it easier to understand. F
classification of dinosaurs and the geological periods are
way that is accessible to the reader.
Some information and descriptions are based on current scientific theories and assumptions.
Visual representations of dinosaurs and other reptiles are artists' visions based on current knowledge.

IMAGES AND ILLUSTRATIONS

All illustrations of dinosaurs and reptiles on pages 22 to 125 (except pages 103, 114 and 126) and pages 134-135 are by:
- Warpaintcobra (istockphoto.com) - all illustrations except those mentioned below.
- Racksuz (istockphoto.com) - for the illustrations on pages 56-57 and 92-93.
- Leonello (istockphoto.com) - for the illustrations on pages 72-73.

All other illustrations were created by various artists from Freepik.com, including AntonioMori, Photographeeasia, Upklyak, Vecstock and many others. Many thanks to them for their work.

Cover illustrations: Warpaintcobra and StockEzy.

Copyright

No part of this book may be reproduced in any form or by any means. The same applies to any distribution, transformation, translation or adaptation.
Any infringement of copyright will be prosecuted in accordance with copyright laws.

© 2023 JOGABOOKS - jogabooks@gmail.com

CONTENT

INTRODUCTION — 4
Life on Earth — 6
Fossils — 8
Paleontology — 10
What is a dinosaur? — 12
Classification — 16
Pangea — 17
The origin of the dinosaurs — 18

DINOSAURS — 20
Achelousaurus — 22
Allosaurus — 24
Altirhinus — 26
Anchisaurus — 28
Ankylosaurus — 30
Apatosaurus — 32
Archaeopteryx — 34
Baryonyx — 36
Brachiosaurus — 38
Camptosaurus — 40
Carnotaurus — 42
Ceratosaurus — 44
Coelophysis — 46
Compsognathus — 48
Crichtonsaurus — 50
Deinonychus — 52
Diabloceratops — 54
Dilophosaurus — 56
Diplodocus — 58
Edmontosaurus — 60
Gargoyleosaurus — 62
Giganotosaurus — 64
Iguanodon — 66
Kentrosaurus — 68

Lambeosaurus	70
Pachycephalosaurus	72
Parasaurolophus	74
Pelecanimimus	76
Placerias	78
Protoceratops	80
Psittacosaurus	82
Pyroraptor	84
Spinophorosaurus	86
Spinosaurus	88
Stegosaurus	90
Therizinosaurus	82
Triceratops	94
Tyrannosaurus	96
Velafrons	98
Velociraptor	100

FLYING REPTILES 102
Anhanguera	104
Dimorphodon	106
Pterodactyl	108
Quetzalcoatlus	110
Thalassodromeus	112

MARINE REPTILES 114
Elasmosaurus	116
Eurhinosaurus	118
Liopleurodon	120
Nothosaurus	122
Tylosaurus	124

EXTINCTION 126
The end of the dinosaurs	128
The legacy of the dinosaurs	132

INTRODUCTION

Dinosaurs appeared on Earth 240 million years ago.

But where did they come from? What do we really know about them?

LIFE ON EARTH

Our planet, Earth, was formed 4.5 billion years ago.

For the first few million years of its existence, the Earth was a planet of molten rock, and temperatures were extremely hot.

Then the Earth began to cool. Its surface hardened, and an atmosphere rich in nitrogen and carbon dioxide appeared. Water, probably brought by comets and meteorites, condensed and formed an immense ocean.

Around 3.8 billion years ago, thanks to the presence of hydrogen, carbon, oxygen and nitrogen, amino acids (molecules essential to the formation of proteins) appeared in the oceans. Scientists call this "primordial soup".

The conditions were thus ripe for the appearance of life.

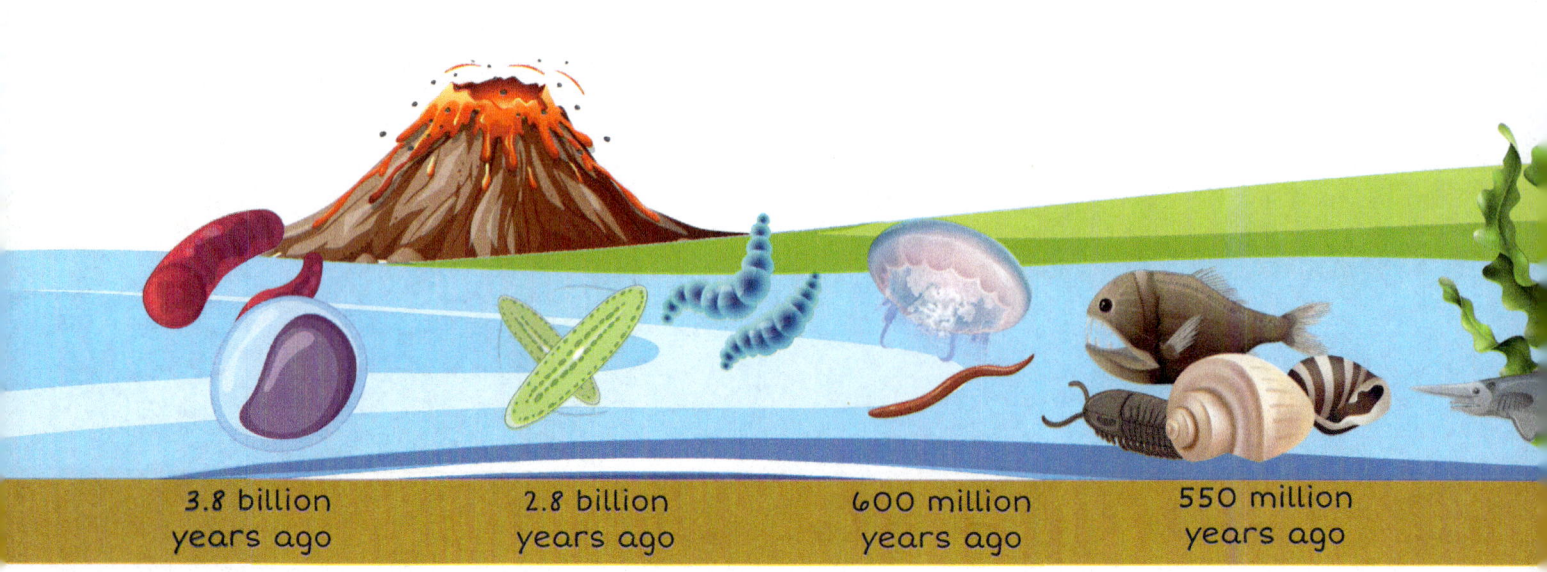

| 3.8 billion years ago | 2.8 billion years ago | 600 million years ago | 550 million years ago |

So, 3.8 billion years ago, the first living beings appeared in the form of bacteria. The first plants (algae) appeared 2.8 billion years ago.

As evolution progressed, living cells became increasingly structured, and the first multi-cellular organisms appeared.

600 million years ago, the first animals appeared, made up of soft bodies resembling jellyfish or worms.

Evolution accelerated 50 million years later, giving rise to a multitude of species, including the trilobite, the first marine vertebrates and the first fish, as well as gastropods (snails, for example).

The first land plants appeared 400 million years ago, along with amphibians and the first insects. The Nautilus also appeared at this time.

The first reptiles appeared 350 million years ago.

The first dinosaurs appeared 240 million years ago, along with the first mammals and turtles.

The first birds appeared 160 million years ago. But 66 million years ago, the dinosaurs disappeared!

| 400 million years ago | 350 million years ago | 250 million years ago | 160 million years ago | 66 million years ago |

FOSSILS

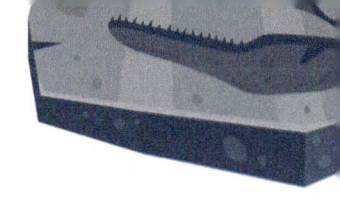

When the dinosaurs disappeared 66 million years ago, humans didn't exist!

In fact, the first humans appeared 2.8 million years ago.

So how did we discover the existence of dinosaurs? How do we know what they looked like, and how they lived?

Thanks to fossils!

A fossil is an ancient trace of life preserved in a natural environment. Simply put, they are the remains of an animal or plant that has been extinct for a very long time.

It can be a whole skeleton or just a piece of bone, but it can also be a footprint or a plant stem or leaf.

Fossils can be found in ice (as in the case of certain mammoths, for example), or in amber (a fossilized plant resin in which insects or small plants can be found). But most fossils form in sedimentary rock.

The formation of a fossil is a slow and complex process, requiring a specific environment.

Most often, a fossil is formed when an animal dies in a wetland (such as a river, beach or marsh) and its body is covered with sediment (such as mud or sand...).

These sediments can be brought in by water (river, ocean, sea, rain, spring...) or, more rarely, by wind (sand, fine earth...).

The soft tissues (skin, muscles, etc.) decompose very quickly, leaving only the animal's skeleton, carapace or shell.

Water and humidity are loaded with minerals (notably calcium) that gradually penetrate the animal's bones. Organic matter is gradually transformed into mineral matter. In simple terms, bone turns to stone.

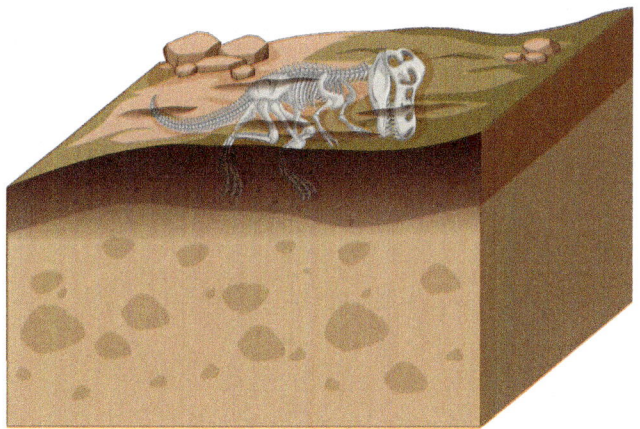

It can also be the case that sediment gradually transforms into rock. In this way, they preserve, for example, the footprint left by an animal as it walks.

PALEONTOLOGY

Paleontology is the scientific discipline that studies living organisms that lived on Earth in ancient times.

Paleontologists study fossils extensively. Sometimes, when the skeleton of a dinosaur is not complete, they have to compare the bones found with those of other dinosaurs, in order to reconstitute the animal in its entirety.

Some dinosaurs have even been reconstructed from a single bone!

To find out when a dinosaur lived, paleontologists rely heavily on the study of sediment layers (or geological strata). Generally speaking, the older the layer, the older the fossil.

In this drawing, the bottom layer corresponds to the Paleozoic era (from the appearance of life on Earth to the appearance of dinosaurs).

The middle layer corresponds to the Mesozoic era (i.e. the era of the dinosaurs), and the top layer corresponds to the Cenozoic era (from the disappearance of the dinosaurs to the present day).

Paleontology is a modern science.

Yet the very first fossils were discovered a very long time ago. Written records from the 6th century BC describe fossilized bones. But back then, people didn't know that these bones were the remains of dinosaurs.

In China, they were even thought to be dragon bones.

In 1677, Robert Plot, an English scientist, discovered a very large piece of femur. He concluded that it belonged to a giant man.

Paleontology took off in the 18th century. Georges Cuvier, a French scientist, developed the concepts of anatomical comparison between species.

In 1824, William Buckland, an English scientist, studied bones and attributed them to a giant lizard, which he named "megalosaurus" (i.e. "great lizard").

In 1825, Gideon Mantell, an English paleontologist, discovered the fossilized teeth of an unknown species. He named it "Iguanodon" (iguana teeth).

In 1842, Richard Owen, a British paleontologist, coined the word "dinosaur". The word comes from the Greek "Deinos" (terrible) and "Sauria" (lizard).

The 19th and 20th centuries saw the discovery of numerous dinosaur skeletons, including Triceratops, Tyrannosaurus and Diplodocus.

But what is a dinosaur?

WHAT IS A DINOSAUR?

For a long time, scientists considered dinosaurs to be reptiles, like lizards for example.

It's true that there are many similarities between them. Today, most specialists believe that dinosaurs are not reptiles.

Dinosaurs and reptiles belong to a large family called the Sauropsids. Put simply, dinosaurs are not reptiles, but they are cousins.

So what is a dinosaur?

Scientists have agreed on some common characteristics of dinosaurs:

- Dinosaurs are terrestrial animals, which excludes flying and marine reptiles.
- Legs are placed under the body and not on the sides (like crocodiles, for example). This explains why many dinosaurs became bipedal.
- The hip bone is characteristic and divided into two groups: Ornithischians (bird hip) and Saurischians (lizard hip).
- Dinosaurs are oviparous: they lay eggs.
- The skull of a dinosaur has 2 orbital windows (two cavities in front of the orbits).
- Dinosaurs have tails of varying lengths.

Scientists have now catalogued more than 1,000 dinosaur species.

Some species are very similar, others very different.

There were carnivorous (meat-eating), herbivorous (plant-eating), piscivorous (fish-eating) and omnivorous (meat and plant-eating) dinosaurs.

Some dinosaurs, often herbivores, swallowed small stones to aid digestion. With the contractions of the stomach, these stones acted like millstones, crushing plants.

These stones are called gastroliths.

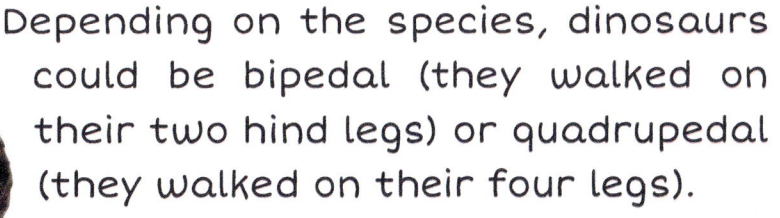

Depending on the species, dinosaurs could be bipedal (they walked on their two hind legs) or quadrupedal (they walked on their four legs).

Until a few decades ago, everyone thought that dinosaurs had skin covered with scales, like lizards.

This is true for some of them. But scientists have also discovered that some dinosaurs had feathers!

They probably weren't totally covered, but had them in places.

Ever since the first dinosaur fossils were discovered, scientists have been asking an important question:

Were dinosaurs warm-blooded or cold-blooded?

Reptiles are cold-blooded animals. In other words, their bodies don't produce heat. That's why lizards, for example, like to lie in the sun. They warm their bodies. The internal temperature of reptiles is therefore not constant and depends on the temperature of their environment.

Mammals, for example (including humans), are warm-blooded animals. In fact, our bodies produce their own heat, which is constant.

Generally speaking, warm-blooded animals need to eat much more than cold-blooded animals. Producing heat requires energy, and therefore more food.

This expenditure of energy is called the metabolic rate. The higher it is, the more energy the animal needs. In conclusion, warm-blooded animals have a higher metabolic rate than cold-blooded animals.

Recently, scientists invented a new method for analyzing bones, and thus deducing the metabolic rate of dinosaurs. According to these scientists, many dinosaurs were warm-blooded animals.

The Saurischians were all warm-blooded dinosaurs.

For the Ornithischians, it all depended on the group. Ornithopods were also warm-blooded, while Thyreophorans and Marginocephalians seem to have reduced their metabolic rate over time to become cold-blooded.

The lifespan of dinosaurs varied greatly from one species to another.

Paleontologists estimate that the smallest dinosaurs had a life expectancy of around 5 or 6 years.

Large carnivores, such as Tyrannosaurus, could live up to 30 years.

The largest dinosaurs, such as Diplodocus, could live to be 80 years old.

CLASSIFICATION

Dinosaurs are classified into 2 main categories, according to the shape of their pelvic bones:

Saurischians and Ornithischians.

The Saurischians (lizard hips) are divided into 2 groups:

- Theropods include all bipedal carnivorous dinosaurs, such as Tyrannosaurus and Velociraptor.

- Sauropodomorphs are herbivorous bipedal or quadrupedal dinosaurs with long necks and tails. Diplodocus belongs to this category.

Ornithischians (bird hips) are divided into 3 groups:

- Ornithopods include bipedal or quadrupedal herbivores, whose feet were shaped like birds' feet (hence their name).

- Thyreophorans include armored herbivorous dinosaurs with bony plates, such as Stegosaurus and Ankylosaurus.

- Marginocephalians are dinosaurs with a bony crest on the skull. This crest, also known as a bony frill, could be flat (like the Triceratops), or domed (like the Pachycephalosaurus).

PANGEA

In the days of the dinosaurs, the Earth was not as we know it today.

Temperatures on the planet's surface were warmer than today and more homogeneous, with an average temperature of 25°C (80°F). The oceans were also warmer, with an average surface temperature of between 25 and 35°C (80 and 95°F).

The fundamental difference between today's planet and that of the dinosaurs was the shape of the continents.

At the time of the first dinosaurs, there was only one continent: Pangea.

This immense continent began to fracture around 300 million years ago, before the appearance of the dinosaurs. But the separation of the continents began 200 million years ago. It would take another 80 million years for Africa and South America to separate.

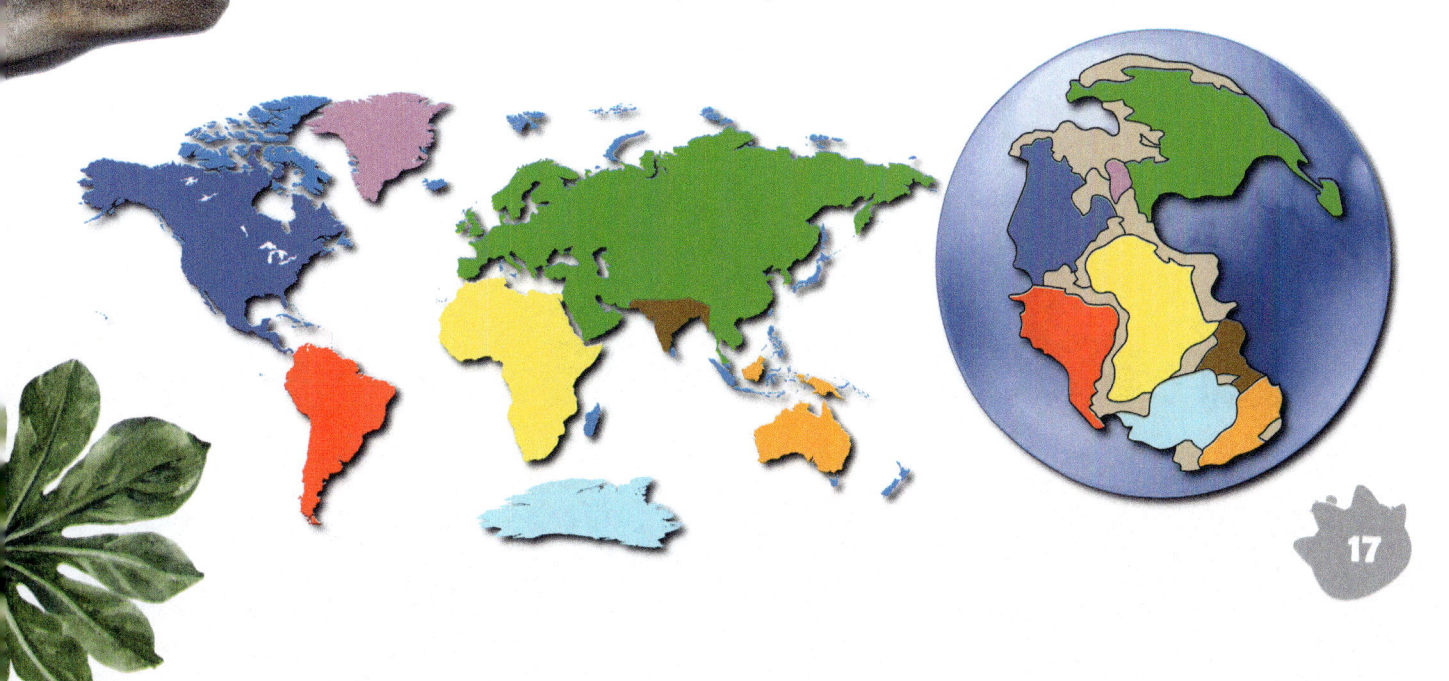

THE ORIGIN OF THE DINOSAURS

250 million years ago, the Earth experienced a mass extinction event.

95% of marine species and 75% of terrestrial species disappeared.

The most likely cause was a gigantic volcanic eruption in present-day Siberia. This event modified the atmosphere, releasing large quantities of gas. Oxygen became scarce, causing the extinction of many plant and animal species within a few thousand years.

This marked the end of the Paleozoic era and the beginning of the Mesozoic era.

The Mesozoic era is divided into 3 periods: Triassic, Jurassic and Cretaceous.

250 million years ago	200 million years ago
TRIASSIC →	JURASSIC

The very first dinosaurs appeared around 240 million years ago, during the Triassic period.

Their appearance was the result of the evolution of certain Archosaurian species (including crocodiles and birds).
At that time, they were still only small, primitive dinosaurs.

The first mammals appeared at the same time.

At the end of the Triassic, another extinction occurred, probably once again due to volcanic activity. Dinosaurs, however, seem unaffected.

During the Jurassic, dinosaur species diversified. This is the period when large dinosaurs appeared.

Dinosaur evolution continued in the Cretaceous, with the appearance of the famous Tyrannosaurus and Triceratops.

145 million years ago

66 million years ago

CRETACEOUS

DINOSAURS

Dinosaurs ruled the Earth for 180 million years.

There were many different species.

Let's discover some of them.

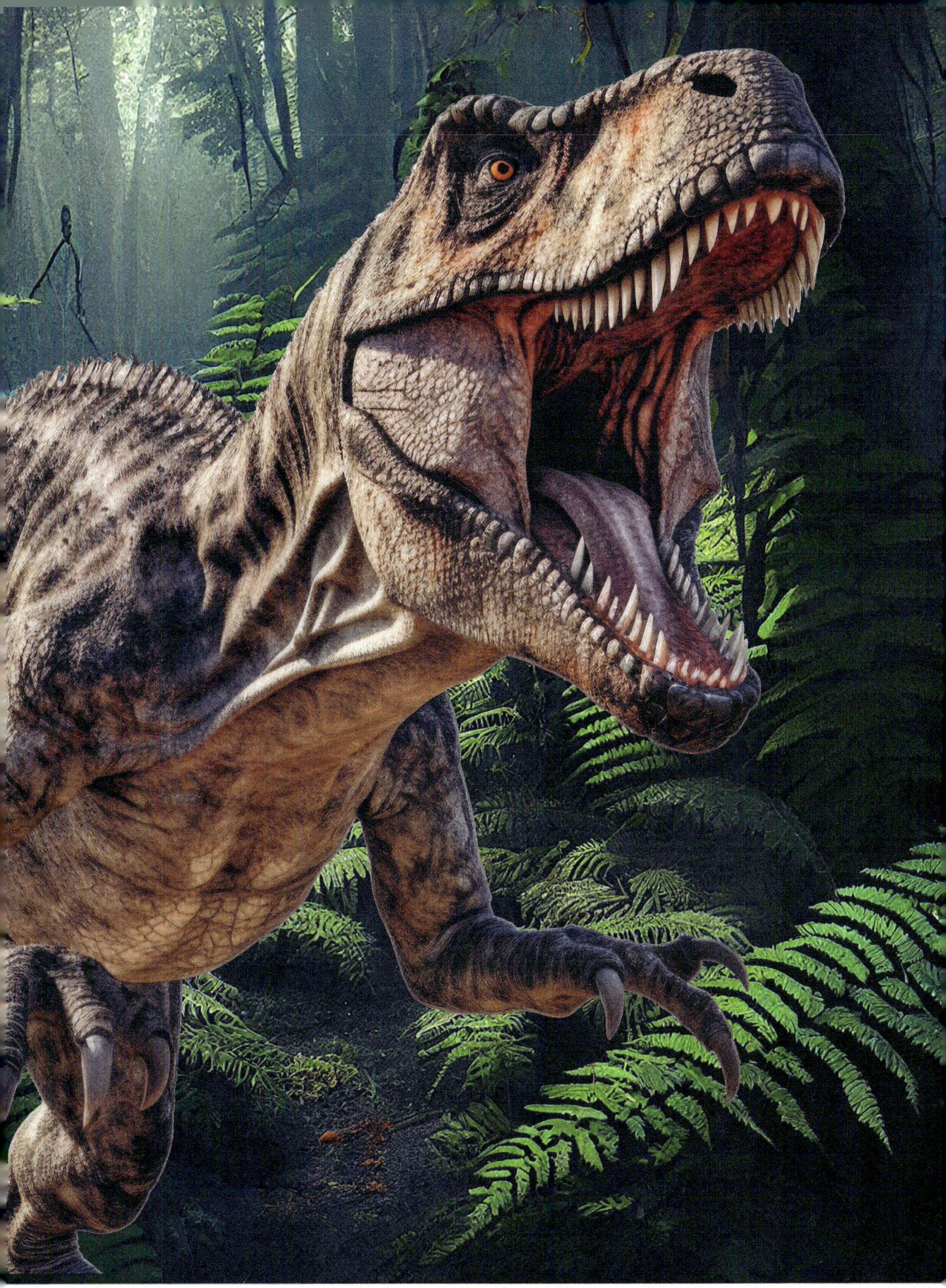

ACHELOUSAURUS

Achelousaurus lived in North America.

It closely resembled the famous Triceratops, and these two dinosaurs were actually related.

However, Achelousaurus had no horns on its nose or forehead.

Achelousaurus had a large bony frill on the back of its skull, and a sort of bony crest on its nose. Above its eyes, too, were prominent bony forms.

Finally, two large horns were located on the back of his bony frill.
The use of these horns remains an enigma. Their position did not allow the Achelousaurus to attack, as it would have had to retract its head between its front legs. It is likely that these horns were used for ceremonial purposes.

FOOD	Herbivorous
CLASSIFICATION	Marginocephalians
PERIOD	Cretaceous
HEIGHT	10 Feet
LENGTH	20 Feet
WEIGHT	8800 Lbs

The first fossil was discovered in 1987 in Montana (USA), but was only studied in 1995.

Achelousaurus means "lizard of Acheloos". Acheloos was a god of Greek mythology. According to legend, he confronted Hercules and lost a horn during the fight. Indeed, the bony bumps on Achelousaurus are reminiscent of severed horns.

ALLOSAURUS

Allosaurus was a Jurassic carnivore. Its imposing size made it a formidable predator.

Its imposing head was surmounted by two bony bumps above its eyes. It is estimated that Allosaurus could run at a speed of 22 MPH.

Allosaurus closely resembled the famous Tyrannosaurus. Yet the two dinosaurs were not exactly related. What's more, the Allosaurus was slightly smaller than the T-Rex.

The first specimen was discovered in 1869 in Colorado, North America. The first people to see this fossil thought it was a petrified horse hoof. In reality, it was a piece of vertebra from the dinosaur's tail.

American paleontologist Othniel Charles Marsh named it Allosaurus in 1877.

In 1991, a 95% complete skeleton was discovered in Wyoming, still in North America. It was a young Allosaurus, 26 feet long. Paleontologists discovered that some of its bones were broken and bore strange marks. It is likely that this dinosaur, nicknamed Big Al by scientists, had died of a bone infection.

In 2005, a study of fossilized Allosaurus bones revealed an injury to a vertebra in the tail. This would have been caused by a blow from the tail of a Stegosaurus. The Allosaurus survived the wound as it showed signs of healing.

Allosaurus means "different lizard".

FOOD	Carnivorous
CLASSIFICATION	Theropods
PERIOD	Jurassic
HEIGHT	17 Feet
LENGTH	40 Feet
WEIGHT	4500 Lbs

ALTIRHINUS

Altirhinus closely resembled another better-known ornithopod dinosaur, Iguanodon.

Both bipedal and quadrupedal, Altirhinus was an imposing herbivore. It lived in what is now Mongolia.

Its thumb was actually a horn, enabling it to defend itself against predators. When walking on all fours, this dinosaur relied on its fingertips, not its palm.

Altirhinus's distinctive feature was its nasal hump.

This hump was an extension of the dinosaur's nasal cavities. Altirhinus certainly used it to emit and amplify sounds, and thus to communicate with its fellow creatures, to warn of danger or to scare off a predator.

It's also possible that this nasal cavity may have amplified Altirhinus' sense of smell.

The first fossil was discovered in 1981 by Serguei Kurzanov, a Russian paleontologist.

Altirhinus means "high nose".

FOOD	Herbivorous
CLASSIFICATION	Ornithopods
PERIOD	Cretaceous
HEIGHT	10 Feet
LENGTH	26 Feet
WEIGHT	8800 Lbs

ANCHISAURUS

Anchisaurus was a small Sauropod, about 6.5 feet long. It was very light, weighing only around 66 lbs.

It lived in North America, in a warm, humid climate that favored abundant vegetation.

This dinosaur could walk in both bipedal and quadrupedal positions.

Paleontologists believe, however, that Anchisaurus moved around on all fours most of the time. Herbivores have a larger digestive tract than carnivores. Anchisaurus must therefore have had a large stomach and intestines. The weight of the digestive system would tend to unbalance the small dinosaur in bipedal position. This is why the quadruped position seems to have been the one most often used by Anchisaurus.

FOOD	Herbivorous
CLASSIFICATION	Sauropodomorphs
PERIOD	Jurassic
HEIGHT	6 Feet
LENGTH	6.5 Feet
WEIGHT	66 Lbs

Each of its hands had a thumb enabling it to grasp and tear plants. This thumb included a large claw, very useful for defending itself against predators.

The first fossil was discovered in 1818 in Connecticut, USA, but was named "Anchisaurus" in 1912.

Anchisaurus means "close reptile".

ANKYLOSAURUS

Ankylosaurus was a dinosaur that lived in warm, humid regions, near rivers or swamps.

Ankylosaurus was a rather peaceful dinosaur, but it was also a real tank. It was unable to run or swim, but its morphology made it difficult to attack.

The first Ankylosaur fossil was discovered in 1906 in North America.

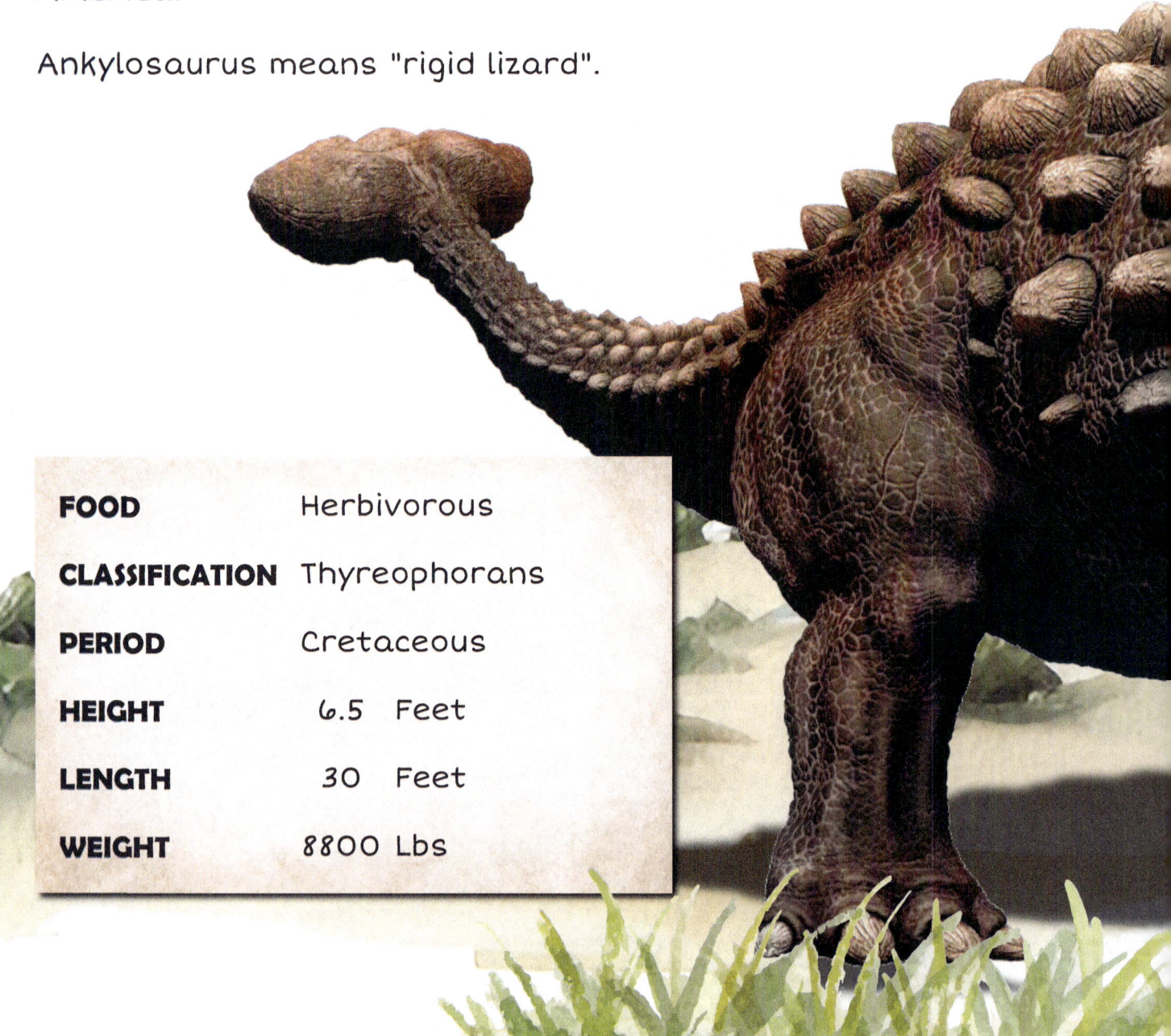

Ankylosaurus means "rigid lizard".

FOOD	Herbivorous
CLASSIFICATION	Thyreophorans
PERIOD	Cretaceous
HEIGHT	6.5 Feet
LENGTH	30 Feet
WEIGHT	8800 Lbs

Ankylosaurus was covered with thick skin. Its back, head and tail were lined with bony plates and spines. Finally, the tip of its tail formed a kind of club made of very compact bones. This weapon alone weighed over 110 lbs.

This defensive armor made Ankylosaurus the dinosaur with the most bones in the world (over a thousand!).

Paleontologists believe that Ankylosaurus could flatten itself on the ground to protect its belly, the only part vulnerable to predators. By swinging its tail, it could easily topple an enemy, even breaking legs or ribs.

APATOSAURUS

Apatosaurus was a gigantic, long-necked herbivore. It lived in present-day North America.

It used its long tail as a weapon to hunt predators. By throwing it with force, it could strike and whip its opponents. The tail was also very important for balance, given the length of its neck.

Apatosaurus was quadrupedal, but could probably stand on its hind legs to reach higher branches. It was a slow-moving dinosaur, walking at an average of 3 MPH. Its feet were wide and cushioned on the underside, rather like those of elephants.

Apatosaurus is at the root of dinosaur species confusion. In 1877, American paleontologist Othniel Charles Marsh studied the bones of a new dinosaur and named it Apatosaurus. Two years later, the same paleontologist, studying other fossils, thought he had discovered a new genus of dinosaur and named it Brontosaurus.

Years later, in 1903, paleontologist Elmer Riggs re-studied the bones and discovered that Brontosaurus and Apatosaurus were in fact the same dinosaur species.
The name "Apatosaurus" was therefore adopted to designate this dinosaur. However, even though the story is old, the name "Brontosaurus" is still remembered. In fact, the US Postal Service issued a stamp with the name Brontosaurus in 1989.

Apatosaurus means "deceptive lizard". The name is not derived from confusion with Brontosaurus, but from the shape of its vertebrae, which resemble those of a marine reptile.

FOOD	Herbivorous
CLASSIFICATION	Sauropodomorphs
PERIOD	Jurassic
HEIGHT	33 Feet
LENGTH	85 Feet
WEIGHT	77 000 Lbs

ARCHAEOPTERYX

Archaeopteryx was a strange dinosaur. So strange, in fact, that scientists wondered about its classification. Even today, some classify it as a dinosaur, others as a bird... because Archaeopteryx was covered in feathers.

What is certain is that Archaeopteryx was a small, light animal with dark plumage.

Birds have brains very similar to those of dinosaurs... But bird brains are much larger. Archaeopteryx had a rather small brain. So the key question is: could it fly, or just glide a short distance? Nobody really knows.

Unlike birds, Archaeopteryx had three long claws on each wing, reptilian dentition and a vertebrate tail.

Archaeopteryx probably fed on insects, small land animals (reptiles, small mammals) and invertebrates (worms, molluscs).

The first fossil was discovered in 1861 in Germany.

Archaeopteryx means "ancient wing".

FOOD	Carnivorous
CLASSIFICATION	Theropods
PERIOD	Jurassic
HEIGHT	20 Inches
LENGTH	24 Inches
WEIGHT	2.2 Lbs

BARYONYX

Baryonyx was a carnivorous dinosaur from the Cretaceous period, living mainly in the regions of today's Western Europe (England, Spain).

Baryonyx was bipedal and had a very distinctive skull. Its head was long, thin and flattened. Its nostrils were not at the tip of its snout, but set back.

Its teeth were larger than those of most carnivorous dinosaurs, acting like daggers to hold down its prey. Baryonyx also had sharp claws, the longest of which measured around 12 inches. It was, however, partly covered with skin. The first fossil, discovered in England in 1983, fascinated the scientific world. Fossilized fish scales were found where its stomach had been, along with a few bones of a very young Iguanodon (a herbivorous dinosaur).

As a result, paleontologists now know exactly what Baryonyx ate.

The shape of its nose, teeth and claws also attest to the fact that this dinosaur ate a lot of fish.

Baryonyx means "heavy claw".

FOOD	Carnivorous
CLASSIFICATION	Theropods
PERIOD	Cretaceous
HEIGHT	13 Feet
LENGTH	39 Feet
WEIGHT	4400 Lbs

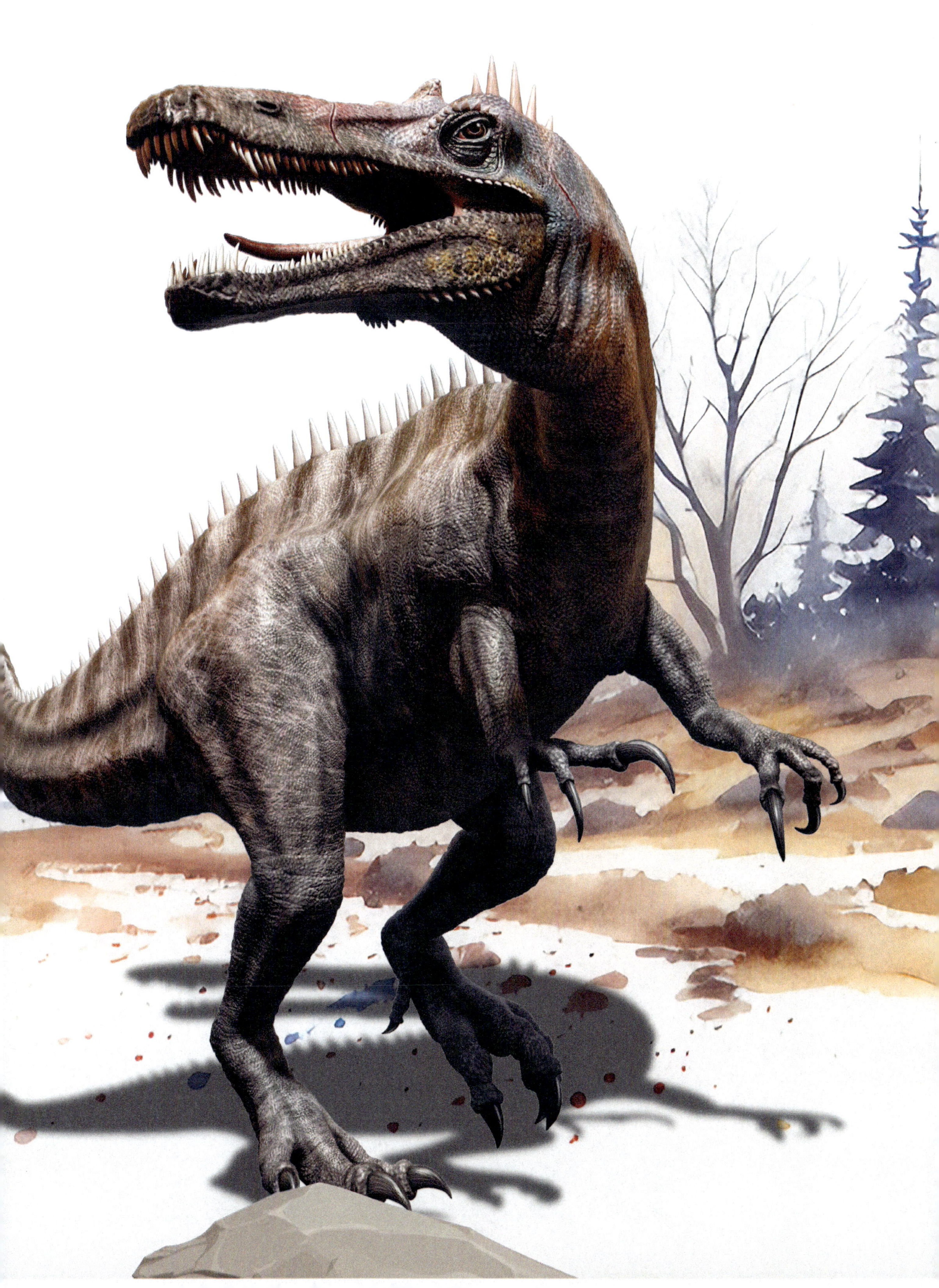

BRACHIOSAURUS

Brachiosaurus was a gigantic dinosaur. It weighed around 88 000 lbs, and could reach a height of almost 50 feet (head and neck erect).

Its neck was made up of 12 vertebrae, each 27 inches long.

Paleontologists believe that Sauropods, of which Brachiosaurus was one, had no stomach. Instead, they had a gizzard, like birds. Finally, their teeth were not used for chewing. They were mainly used for plucking leaves from branches.

For a long time, scientists thought that Brachiosaurus lived most of its life underwater. Indeed, its nostrils are located at the top of its skull. But we now know that living in water was impossible for this dinosaur. Given its size, water pressure would have blocked its breathing. In fact, Brachiosaurus lived mainly on plains and in coniferous forests.

The first Brachiosaurus fossil was discovered in 1900 in Colorado, North America, by Elmer S. Riggs.

Brachiosaurus means "lizard with arms".

FOOD	Herbivorous
CLASSIFICATION	Sauropodomorphs
PERIOD	Jurassic - Cretaceous
HEIGHT	49 Feet
LENGTH	82 Feet
WEIGHT	88 200 Lbs

CAMPTOSAURUS

Camptosaurus was in the same family as the Iguanodon.

It should not be confused with the Camposaurus, which was a small carnivorous dinosaur.

Camptosaurus was a massive herbivore.

The size of its stomach was relatively large for its size.
This is explained by the fact that Camptosaurus ate tough leaves and branches, which were difficult to digest.

This dinosaur was bipedal. Its forelimbs (i.e. its arms) did not allow it to move around, but could nevertheless support its weight so that it could eat plants at ground level.

Analysis of its bones shows that its tendons were extremely strong. In most animals, including dinosaurs, tendons, which enable muscles to cling to bones, are tough but flexible.

Camptosaurus tendons, as the dinosaur aged, tended to calcify, i.e. turn into bone.

The first Camptosaurus fossil was discovered in England in 1874.

Camptosaurus means "flexible reptile".

FOOD	Herbivorous
CLASSIFICATION	Ornithopods
PERIOD	Jurassic - Cretaceous
HEIGHT	16.5 Feet
LENGTH	20 Feet
WEIGHT	8800 Lbs

CARNOTAURUS

Carnotaurus was a medium-sized carnivore, smaller than the Tyrannosaurus.

Its arms were very atrophied indeed, and surprisingly small for a dinosaur of its size.

His teeth were also finer than those of other predators of his rank. It was therefore impossible for him to bite into bones that were too large without breaking his teeth. However, analyses of its jaws revealed that it was capable of biting with a very rapid movement.
Paleontologists also believe that Carnotaurus could run very fast, with a top speed of over 30 MPH.

It is therefore likely that the Carnotaurus preyed on relatively small (thin-boned), fast-moving prey.

Two bony growths protruded from its skull above the eyes. These horns, however, were far too small to be used as a defense or to attack prey.

Carnotaurus was discovered in Argentina in 1985 by José Bonaparte, an Argentine paleontologist.

This discovery was of great interest to the scientific community: firstly, the skeleton found was almost complete, which is quite rare. Secondly, the dinosaur's skin left traces in the rock, like an impression or a mold. As a result, scientists were able to see that Carnotaurus had a skin covered with scales, like a modern-day reptile.

Carnotaurus means "carnivorous bull".

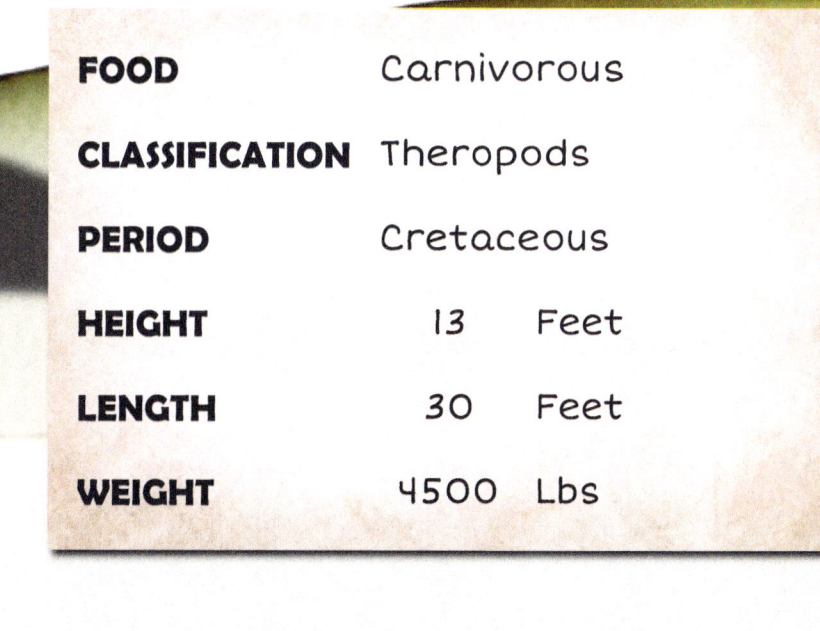

FOOD	Carnivorous
CLASSIFICATION	Theropods
PERIOD	Cretaceous
HEIGHT	13 Feet
LENGTH	30 Feet
WEIGHT	4500 Lbs

CERATOSAURUS

Ceratosaurus was a bipedal carnivore that lived in North America.

Ceratosaurus was rather modest in size for a Jurassic carnivore. Unlike Allosaurus and Tyrannosaurus, it was unable to attack large prey.

It preyed mainly on Ornithopods and small Sauropods.

A distinctive feature of this dinosaur was a small, rounded horn on its nose, located just behind the nostrils. It also had two small bony ridges above the eyes. Study of its bones shows that it had a sturdier neck than other carnivores of the same era.

This suggests that Ceratosaurus could pounce on its prey at full speed and stun them with a headbutt.

Another interesting difference is that Ceratosaurus had four fingers on each hand, whereas other theropods generally had three.

The first Ceratosaurus fossil was discovered in 1883.

Ceratosaurus means "horned lizard".

FOOD	Carnivorous
CLASSIFICATION	Theropods
PERIOD	Jurassic
HEIGHT	10 Feet
LENGTH	20 Feet
WEIGHT	2200 Lbs

COELOPHYSIS

Cœlophysis was a small, primitive dinosaur from the Triassic period.

Cœlophysis was light and very fast. It could reach speeds of up to 28 MPH. Its lightness was due to its skeleton, whose bones were hollow.

The first fossils were discovered in New Mexico in 1881 by David Baldwin, an American paleontologist.
In 1947, excavations were carried out at the same site, resulting in an astonishing discovery: The remains of some twenty different skeletons, probably all drowned in a flash flood.

This discovery established with certainty that Cœlophysis lived in groups.

Given its size, the Cœlophysis, even if it hunted in packs, could not attack large prey. Its diet consisted of small reptiles or mammals, insects and small aquatic animals (frogs, fish...)...

But Cœlophysis was also a cannibal!

Fossilized skeletons of very young Cœlophysis were discovered inside adult Cœlophysis skeletons. Paleontologists first thought that this dinosaur was ovoviviparous. Ovoviviparous are animals whose eggs hatch in their bellies, like some vipers. But given the size of the young skeletons, far too large to be contained in an egg, scientists concluded that Cœlophysis sometimes ate their offspring.

Cœlophysis means "hollow form", in reference to the structure of its bones.

FOOD	Carnivorous
CLASSIFICATION	Theropods
PERIOD	Triassic
HEIGHT	5 Feet
LENGTH	10 Feet
WEIGHT	45 Lbs

COMPSOGNATHUS

Compsognathus was a tiny carnivorous dinosaur from the Jurassic period.

It lived in tropical climates, near coastal regions.

Its small size and light weight enabled it to reach high speeds of around 40 MPH. For a bipedal animal, this speed is exceptional. Today, the ostrich is the only bipedal animal capable of reaching this speed.

Compsognathus fed on small reptiles, mammals, insects and eggs. In fact, the skeleton of a lizard was discovered inside a Compsognathus fossil.

It had a slender jaw and sharp, pointed teeth. Its eyes were relatively well-developed for the size of its skull, giving it excellent vision.

Only two Compsognathus fossils have been found to date: The first in Germany in 1850 and the other in France in 1972.

Compsognathus means "delicate jaw".

FOOD	Carnivorous
CLASSIFICATION	Theropods
PERIOD	Jurassic
HEIGHT	24 Inches
LENGTH	55 Inches
WEIGHT	6.5 Lbs

CRICHTONSAURUS

Crichtonsaurus was a dinosaur in the same family as Ankylosaurus, but smaller.

It is a recently discovered species. The first fossil was discovered in 2002, in China.

Not much is known about this dinosaur at present.

It is very likely that, like Ankylosaurus, Crichtonsaurus had a bony club at the end of its tail. However, its overall morphology and size suggest that this club could not have been as heavy as that of Ankylosaurus.

FOOD	Herbivorous
CLASSIFICATION	Thyreophorans
PERIOD	Cretaceous
HEIGHT	5 Feet
LENGTH	11 Feet
WEIGHT	1200 Lbs

Crichtonsaurus was a robust dinosaur, its back covered with bony structures resembling vertically placed plates. Its skull was also armored, and it had two pairs of small horns on the back of its head, at cheek and eye socket level.

Crichtonsaurus had a powerful beak, enabling it to feed on tough vegetation such as roots and branches.

Crichtonsaurus means "Crichton's lizard". Paleontologists named this dinosaur after Michael Crichton, author of the "Jurassic Park" books.

DEINONYCHUS

Deinonychus was a modestly sized but formidable predator.

Its morphology enabled it to reach speeds of over 22 MPH, and to have sufficient agility to pounce on its prey. Its arms were relatively long for a dinosaur of its species. The shape of its humerus suggests that Deinonychus had great upper limb strength.

It also had a long, crescent-shaped claw on the second toe of each foot. This weapon enabled it to lacerate its prey. In fact, analysis of its jaws and teeth shows that Deinonychus could not kill by biting. So it was this claw that enabled it to attack and kill.

Analysis of its skull shows that this dinosaur had a fairly large, well-developed brain.

Paleontologists believe that Deinonychus' intelligence enabled it to adopt organized social behaviors, such as developing pack hunting strategies. Such an ability enabled these dinosaurs to attack prey much larger than themselves.

The first Deinonychus fossils were discovered in 1931 in Montana, North America. However, these relics were set aside and Deinonychus was not really studied until 1964.

Deinonychus means "terrible claw".

FOOD	Carnivorous
CLASSIFICATION	Theropods
PERIOD	Cretaceous
HEIGHT	6 Feet
LENGTH	11 Feet
WEIGHT	155 Lbs

DIABLOCERATOPS

Diabloceratops was a Cretaceous herbivorous dinosaur found in North America.

At the time, these regions were vast plains dotted with lakes and rivers. Diabloceratops fed on terrestrial and aquatic vegetation and lived in herds.

Like many Marginocephalian dinosaurs, Diabloceratops had a large bony frill at the back of its skull to protect its neck.

He had a small, barely visible horn on his nose and two larger horns above his eyes. His bony frill also had two horns, much longer than the others.

FOOD	Herbivorous
CLASSIFICATION	Marginocephalians
PERIOD	Cretaceous
HEIGHT	6.5 Feet
LENGTH	20 Feet
WEIGHT	4500 Lbs

Its resemblance to the Triceratops is quite remarkable. However, Diabloceratops was much smaller.

The first Diabloceratops fossils were discovered in 1998, but only studied in 2010.

Diabloceratops means "horn-headed devil".

DILOPHOSAURUS

Dilophosaurus lived in North America and Asia.

This medium-sized carnivore had a morphology that enabled it to be agile and fast. It probably used its hind legs to strike its prey, its hands to hold it and its teeth to kill it.

Above all, Dilophosaurus had an astonishing peculiarity: It had a double crest at the top of its skull. Its V-shaped bony appendages could not have been used to strike blows, given their fragility.

Paleontologists therefore believe that this was a sign of recognition, and perhaps a sexual signal during mating season.

Dilophosaurus is often depicted with membranes stretched out on either side of its head. In reality, it's highly unlikely that this is a realistic representation.

This interpretation comes from the film "Jurassic Park" (Steven Spielberg - 1993). At the beginning of the film, a Dilophosaurus appears and chases one of the park's employees. It spits venom in his face and deploys its membranes. All this is an invention for the purposes of the film, and there is no evidence to suggest that this dinosaur had these abilities.

The first Dilophosaurus was discovered in 1942 in the USA.

Dilophosaurus means "two-crested lizard".

FOOD	Carnivorous
CLASSIFICATION	Theropods
PERIOD	Jurassic
HEIGHT	8 Feet
LENGTH	20 Feet
WEIGHT	990 Lbs

DIPLODOCUS

Like all Sauropods, Diplodocus had a very long neck and tail.

It was a true giant!

The top of its back could reach twenty feet in height. But if he straightened his neck, the Diplodocus could easily reach a height of forty feet.

However, this position must have been tiring for him, and most of the time he moved with his neck in a horizontal position.

Diplodocus was a large, harmless herbivore, yet it had a very effective weapon. Its long, slender tail was packed with powerful muscles. By swinging it at high speed, the Diplodocus could whip its opponent.

For a long time, we mistakenly thought that the Diplodocus tail was so heavy that it dragged on the ground when it moved, but this is not true. Powerful ligaments enabled the dinosaur to keep its tail upright, preventing it from dragging its weight around.

The first Diplodocus fossil was discovered in 1877 in North America. It was considered the world's longest dinosaur, until the discovery of Argentinosaurus (a Sauropod discovered in Argentina in 1987 and measuring 116 feet long), then Patagotitan (another Sauropod discovered in 2014 in Patagonia and measuring almost 131 feet long).

Diplodocus means "double beam".

FOOD	Herbivorous
CLASSIFICATION	Sauropodomorphs
PERIOD	Jurassic
HEIGHT	40 Feet
LENGTH	100 Feet
WEIGHT	45 000 Lbs

EDMONTOSAURUS

Edmontosaurus was a herbivore of the late Cretaceous. Mostly quadrupedal, it could nevertheless stand up on its hind legs to feed.

Scientists believe it was also able to run on its two hind legs alone, and at high speed despite its size. Recent biomechanical studies estimate this speed at 30 MPH, twice as fast as a Tyrannosaurus.

Edmontosaurus certainly ate tough, hardy plants. It had a beak to cut plants, and teeth to crush them. Chewing wore down its teeth prematurely, but this dinosaur was perfectly adapted to the task. Edmontosaurus' teeth fell out as they wore down, to be replaced by new ones.

Edmontosaurus' thick skin was covered with small scales, as evidenced by some fossils found with skin impressions (traces of skin left in the rock).

The first fossil was officially discovered in 1917 by Lawrence Morris Lambe, a Canadian paleontologist, in the Horseshoe Canyon region, near the city of Edmonton (Canada). Prior to this date, a number of fossils that might have belonged to Edmontosaurus had been discovered, but some were lost, and others could not be classified due to their poor condition.

Edmontosaurus means "Edmonton reptile".

FOOD	Herbivorous
CLASSIFICATION	Ornithopods
PERIOD	Cretaceous
HEIGHT	13 Feet
LENGTH	43 Feet
WEIGHT	7800 Lbs

GARGOYLEOSAURUS

Like all dinosaurs in the Thyreophorans family, the Gargoyleosaurus was an armored dinosaur. It lived in the regions of present-day North America.

The Gargoyleosaurus was in the same family as the Ankylosaurus. Like Ankylosaurus, it was covered with bony plates and spikes.

It was smaller, however, and did not have a club at the end of its tail. So the dinosaur couldn't really defend itself. Its armour was also less effective, particularly on the flanks (ribs and belly).

It should be noted that the Gargoyleosaurus lived in the Jurassic, while the Ankylosaurus lived in the Cretaceous, and these two periods are separated by several million years. The Ankylosaurus, logically, was more evolved and had a more effective armour.

The first Gargoyleosaurus fossil was discovered in 1996 in Wyoming (USA).

Gargoyleosaurus means "gargoyle lizard", because its skull resembles the gargoyle statues found in many cathedrals.

FOOD	Herbivorous
CLASSIFICATION	Thyreophorans
PERIOD	Jurassic
HEIGHT	3 Feet
LENGTH	10 Feet
WEIGHT	2200 Lbs

GIGANOTOSAURUS

Giganotosaurus was the second-largest carnivorous dinosaur in existence, just behind the Spinosaurus and ahead of the Tyrannosaurus.

Giganotosaurus lived in present-day South America (Argentina, Patagonia).

This dinosaur's hind legs were powerful. It could reach speeds of 30 MPH when hunting.

The first fossil was discovered in 1993 by Ruben Carolini, a fossil collector.

Fossils of Iguanodons and large Sauropods have been found at the same dig sites. It would therefore be logical to assume that Giganotosaurus preyed on large prey.

Some paleontologists have speculated that Giganotosaurus sometimes hunted in packs, precisely in order to kill prey much larger than themselves. However, there is no scientific evidence to support this hypothesis.

Giganotosaurus means "giant southern lizard".

FOOD	Carnivorous
CLASSIFICATION	Theropods
PERIOD	Cretaceous
HEIGHT	21 Feet
LENGTH	46 Feet
WEIGHT	20 000 Lbs

IGUANODON

Iguanodon was one of the first dinosaurs to be discovered.

It lived in warm, humid areas during the Cretaceous period, and was both bipedal and quadrupedal, depending on its environment.

In 1878, some 30 Iguanodon skeletons were discovered in a coal mine in Belgium. It is therefore certain that these dinosaurs lived in groups.

Iguanodon had very specific hands:
Its thumb was a kind of bone spade. It was most likely used for self-defence, striking opponents from below, in the stomach or throat.
The three middle fingers were very wide. Paleontologists believe that when Iguanodon moved on its four legs, it placed only the tips of these three fingers on the ground, rather than the whole palm of the hand.
Finally, its little finger was articulated in such a way that it could be folded towards the palm, like a thumb.
In this way, Iguanodon could grasp plants and pluck them with its hands.

Many Iguanodon fossils have been discovered around the world. Most come from Europe (England, France, Belgium, Spain), but some have been found in the USA, Thailand, Mongolia and Morocco.

Iguanodon means "iguana tooth".

FOOD	Herbivorous
CLASSIFICATION	Ornithopods
PERIOD	Cretaceous
HEIGHT	16.5 Feet
LENGTH	36 Feet
WEIGHT	11 000 Lbs

KENTROSAURUS

Kentrosaurus closely resembled the famous Stegosaurus. In fact, both dinosaurs belonged to the same family.

The Kentrosaurus was essentially quadrupedal. It could, however, stand on its hind legs to pick foliage from higher ground.

Like the Stegosaurus, the Kentrosaurus' back was covered with bony plates. These plates served not only to protect the dinosaur, but also to regulate its temperature.

In addition to the plates, this dinosaur also had large spines, from the middle of its back to the tip of its tail. It also had two other bony spines on its shoulders.

The bony spines on the back, the largest of which were 28 inches long, were purely defensive, but Kentrosaurus could also inflict serious injuries with those on its tail.

Paleontologists estimate that this dinosaur could strike (by swinging its tail) at a speed of around 30 MPH.

Kentrosaurus lived in what is now Africa, and was discovered in 1915.

Kentrosaurus means "spiked lizard".

FOOD	Herbivorous
CLASSIFICATION	Thyreophorans
PERIOD	Jurassic
HEIGHT	6.5 Feet
LENGTH	16.5 Feet
WEIGHT	3300 Lbs

LAMBEOSAURUS

Lambeosaurus was a herbivorous dinosaur found in present-day North America (Canada, USA, Mexico).

This dinosaur was both bipedal and quadrupedal. Its hands were made up of three fingers fused together and a fourth, movable finger that could be used to close the hand and catch foliage.

Lambeosaurus had a distinctive bony crest at the top of its skull. This crest was composed of two forms: an axe-shaped crest on top of the skull, and a bony shaft at the back.

This crest was partly hollow, and the dinosaur's nasal cavities communicated with its throat via this crest.

Paleontologists believe that Lambeosaurus was able to emit and amplify sounds through this bony appendage, probably to communicate with its fellow creatures or attract a sexual partner during mating periods.

The first Lambeosaurus fossil was discovered in 1913 by Charles H. Sternberg, a fossil collector. It was Canadian paleontologist William Parks who named it Lambeosaurus, after Lawrence Lambe, another Canadian paleontologist who first studied the fossil.

FOOD	Herbivorous
CLASSIFICATION	Ornithopods
PERIOD	Cretaceous
HEIGHT	10 Feet
LENGTH	30 Feet
WEIGHT	9000 Lbs

PACHYCEPHALOSAURUS

Pachycephalosaurus lived in present-day North America during the Cretaceous period.

What makes this herbivorous dinosaur so special is its skull.

The skull of Pachycephalosaurus had a bony cap at the top, surrounded by outgrowths resembling small horns.

Paleontologists have long wondered what purpose this bony helmet served.

Obviously, Pachycephalosaurus could have used its skull to defend itself and ward off predators. However, the rest of its body is unprotected (like that of Ankylosaurus, for example). Faced with a large predator, head blows would have been ineffective.

FOOD	Herbivorous
CLASSIFICATION	Marginocephalians
PERIOD	Cretaceous
HEIGHT	6.5 Feet
LENGTH	16.5 Feet
WEIGHT	1100 Lbs

The most likely hypothesis is that Pachycephalosaurus used its skull to fight other dinosaurs, particularly during breeding periods, in the manner of rams for example.

However, analysis of the structure of the skull bones and cervical vertebrae shows that the dinosaur would not have been able to sustain violent blows. Paleontologists therefore believe that these dinosaurs struck each other on the flanks (ribs, belly).

Pachycephalosaurus means "thick-headed lizard".

PARASAUROLOPHUS

Parasaurolophus was a herbivorous dinosaur from the Cretaceous period.

It was both bipedal and quadrupedal, with a mouth shaped like a duck's beak.

It had a very distinctive head shape. This dinosaur had a bony crest at the top of its skull, which extended backwards. This crest could reach a total length of almost seven feet and was in direct contact with the dinosaur's nasal cavity. For a long time, scientists thought it could be used for defense (a bit like a horn), or as a snorkel for underwater breathing.

In reality, the crest was a kind of musical instrument. Acting as a sounding board, it amplified the sounds produced by the dinosaur. In this way, the Parasaurolophus could be heard from a great distance, to communicate with its fellow dinosaurs, to scare off enemies, or for courtship.

In 2010, a baby Parasaurolophus was discovered in Utah (USA). The baby was less than seven feet long and had only a tiny crest. Scientists have therefore deduced that the crests of these dinosaurs grew continuously throughout their lives.

The first Parasaurolophus fossil was discovered in Canada, North America, in 1920.

Parasaurolophus means "close to the crested lizard". In fact, Parasaurolophus is very close to Saurolophus, discovered a little earlier in 1912.

FOOD	Herbivorous
CLASSIFICATION	Ornithopods
PERIOD	Cretaceous
HEIGHT	20 Feet
LENGTH	33 Feet
WEIGHT	11 000 Lbs

PELECANIMIMUS

Pelecanimimus looked like an ostrich!

This dinosaur had an elongated, narrow head, and a small bony crest on the back of its skull.

Pelecanimimus was the theropod with the most teeth. It had 220. These teeth were very small, and their shape suggests that this small dinosaur was omnivorous (it ate both meat and vegetables).

Pelecanimimus also had an extensible membrane under its throat, like pelicans. The dinosaur's, however, was much smaller.

Paleontologists believe that Pelecanimimus fed in shallow water near rivers and lakes. Walking through the water, as a heron would, Pelecanimus caught small fish or amphibians (such as frogs or salamanders) and stored them in its neck pouch.

It's also possible that this pouch played a role during the mating period, as it does for some birds that inflate their throats to attract a mate.

The one and only Pelecanimimus fossil in existence today was discovered in Spain.

Pelecanimimus means "imitating a pelican".

FOOD	Omnivorous
CLASSIFICATION	Theropods
PERIOD	Cretaceous
HEIGHT	5 Feet
LENGTH	7 Feet
WEIGHT	55 Lbs

PLACERIAS

Placerias was not a dinosaur in the scientific sense. But its atypical morphology deserves attention.

Placerias lived in the Triassic period, and thus cohabited with numerous dinosaur species.
It is in fact a reptile, belonging to the Dicynodont family (meaning "with two dog teeth").

These herbivores lived all over the continent (Pangea), travelling in large herds of hundreds of individuals.

Since Triassic dinosaurs were small in size, the Placerias was the largest herbivore of this era.

It lived in very wet areas, near rivers. Paleontologists estimate that this reptile spent most of its time in the water, much like a hippopotamus.

Its sharp beak and two large teeth were used to search the ground for food.

Its skull was massive, with a small bony frill at the back.

In 1930, American paleontologists Charles Lewis Camp and Samuel Paul Welles discovered some forty Placerias fossils in Arizona, North America.

FOOD	Herbivorous
CLASSIFICATION	Dicynodont
PERIOD	Triassic
HEIGHT	3 Feet
LENGTH	11 Feet
WEIGHT	2200 Lbs

PROTOCERATOPS

Protoceratops was a small herbivorous dinosaur belonging to the Marginocephalian dinosaur family. It is even highly probable that it was the ancestor of the Triceratops.

Protoceratops had no horns, but it did have a slight bony protrusion on its nose. It had a large bony frill protecting its neck. The size of this crest seems to have depended on the sex of the dinosaur. Males had a more developed frill than females.
Its beak, in front of its mouth, was powerful and could cut through strong branches. Its large teeth enabled it to crush even the toughest vegetation.

Protoceratops lived in herds in arid desert regions. Paleontologists believe it fed by searching the ground with its beak, looking for roots and other buried vegetation.

The first Protoceratops fossil was discovered in 1922 in Mongolia, Asia.

Protoceratops means "first horned head".

FOOD	Herbivorous
CLASSIFICATION	Marginocephalians
PERIOD	Jurassic
HEIGHT	3 Feet
LENGTH	7 Feet
WEIGHT	330 Lbs

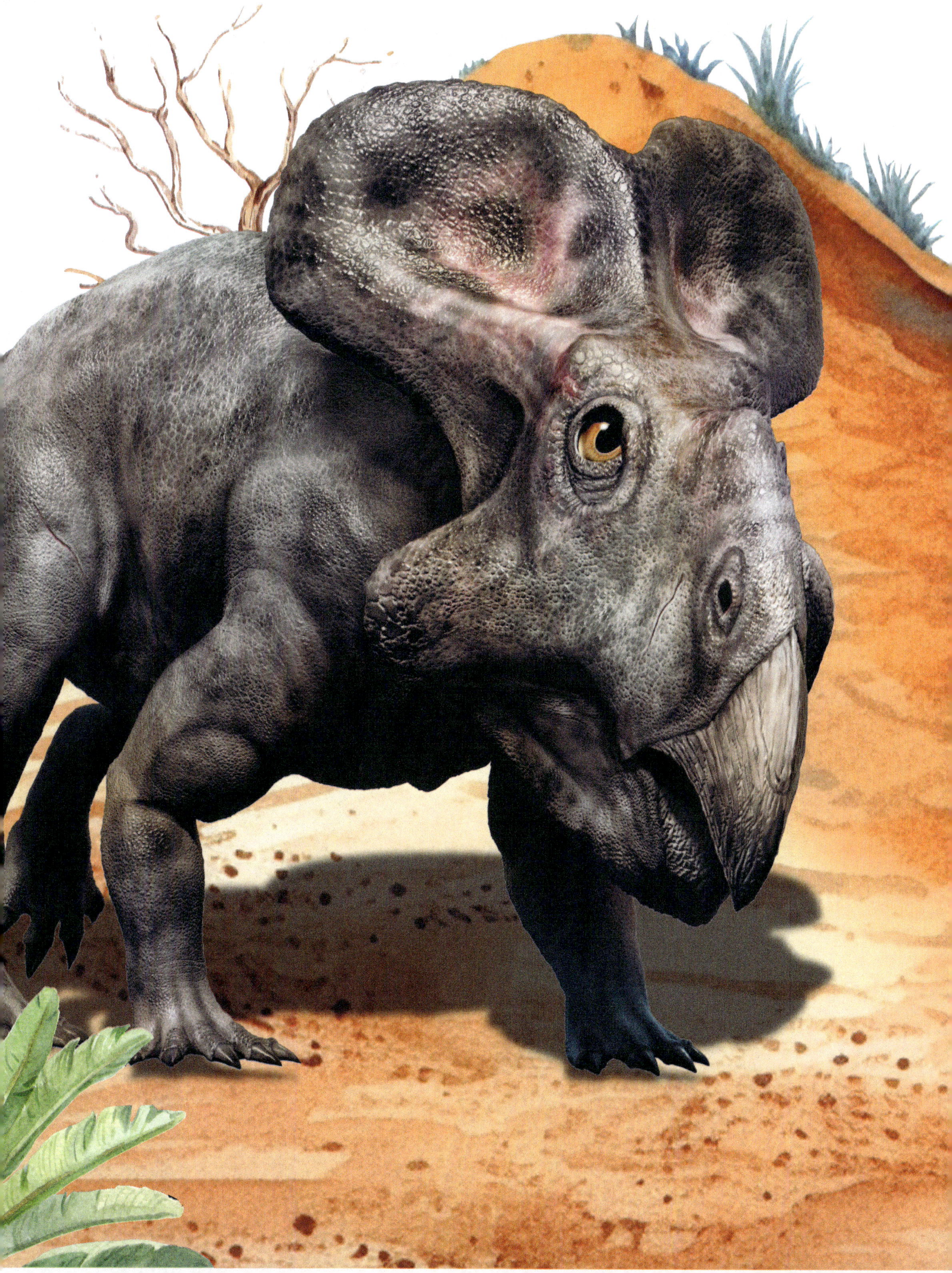

PSITTACOSAURUS

Psittacosaurus was a small herbivorous dinosaur that lived in the early Cretaceous period in the regions of present-day Asia (China, Siberia, Mongolia).

This dinosaur was a primitive Ceratopsian (i.e. a distant ancestor of dinosaurs such as Triceratops).

The back of its skull had a tiny, almost invisible bony frill. Its cheek bones formed two small horns.

Psittacosaurus was bipedal and quadrupedal. To escape from danger, it could run quickly on its hind legs. To feed, or move about more peacefully, it used all four legs. It also used its front legs to find food in the ground.

Its powerful beak enabled it to cut tough vegetation. Amazingly, its lower jaw was able to slide back and forth. This enabled the dinosaur to crush vegetation more easily.

Many Psittacosaur fossils contained small stones in their stomachs (gastroliths).

The first Psittacosaurus fossil was discovered in 1923 by Henry Fairfield Osborn, an American paleontologist.

Psittacosaurus means "parrot lizard".

FOOD	Herbivorous
CLASSIFICATION	Marginocephalians
PERIOD	Cretaceous
HEIGHT	3 Feet
LENGTH	6 Feet
WEIGHT	55 Lbs

PYRORAPTOR

Pyroraptor was a small, bipedal, carnivorous dinosaur.

It was in the same family as the Velociraptor and Deinonychus.

The dinosaur's dentition prevented it from breaking strong bones.

Its morphology indicates that Pyroraptor was a fast, agile hunter.

It preyed mainly on small animals, such as small mammals and reptiles. Its sharp claws, on both upper and lower limbs, enabled it to grip and tear small prey.

FOOD	Carnivorous
CLASSIFICATION	Theropods
PERIOD	Cretaceous
HEIGHT	2 Feet
LENGTH	5 Feet
WEIGHT	66 Lbs

It is also likely that it fed on eggs when it found a nest. Pyroraptor's claws were capable of scratching the ground and digging up dinosaur and reptile eggs.

Paleontologists believe that Pyroraptors lived and hunted in small groups.

The only Pyroraptor fossil was discovered in France in 1989. It was a forest fire that led to its discovery, as the fire brought the bones to light.

Pyroraptor means "thief of fire".

SPINOPHOROSAURUS

Spinophorosaurus was a Sauropod, like the famous Diplodocus.

It was, however, half its size, despite being 43 feet long.

This dinosaur most probably lived in herds in the African region.

Spinophorosaurus' distinctive feature was its tail, which had four long, sharp bone spikes at the end.

When attacked, it could deliver a powerful blow to its adversary. The mobility of its caudal vertebrae (i.e., the vertebrae of its tail) enabled it to strike low to the ground or several meters into the air.

Spinophorosaurus was one of the few Sauropods to possess such a weapon.

Spinophorosaurus was discovered in 2009 in Niger, Africa.

Spinophorosaurus means "thorn-bearing lizard".

FOOD	Herbivorous
CLASSIFICATION	Sauropodomorphs
PERIOD	Jurassic
HEIGHT	20 Feet
LENGTH	43 Feet
WEIGHT	15 500 Lbs

SPINOSAURUS

Spinosaurus lived in the Cretaceous regions of North Africa and the Middle East.

Spinosaurus was a fearsome predator, probably the largest of the carnivorous dinosaurs. Thanks to its morphology, it could reach speeds of up to 25 MPH.

Its elongated jaws and sharp teeth enabled it to hunt both terrestrial and aquatic prey, such as fish and marine reptiles.

Its back featured long bony spines over six feet high, covered with skin stretched to form a sail. Paleontologists still wonder about the precise function of this organ: Thermal regulator? Courtship? Protection against predators?

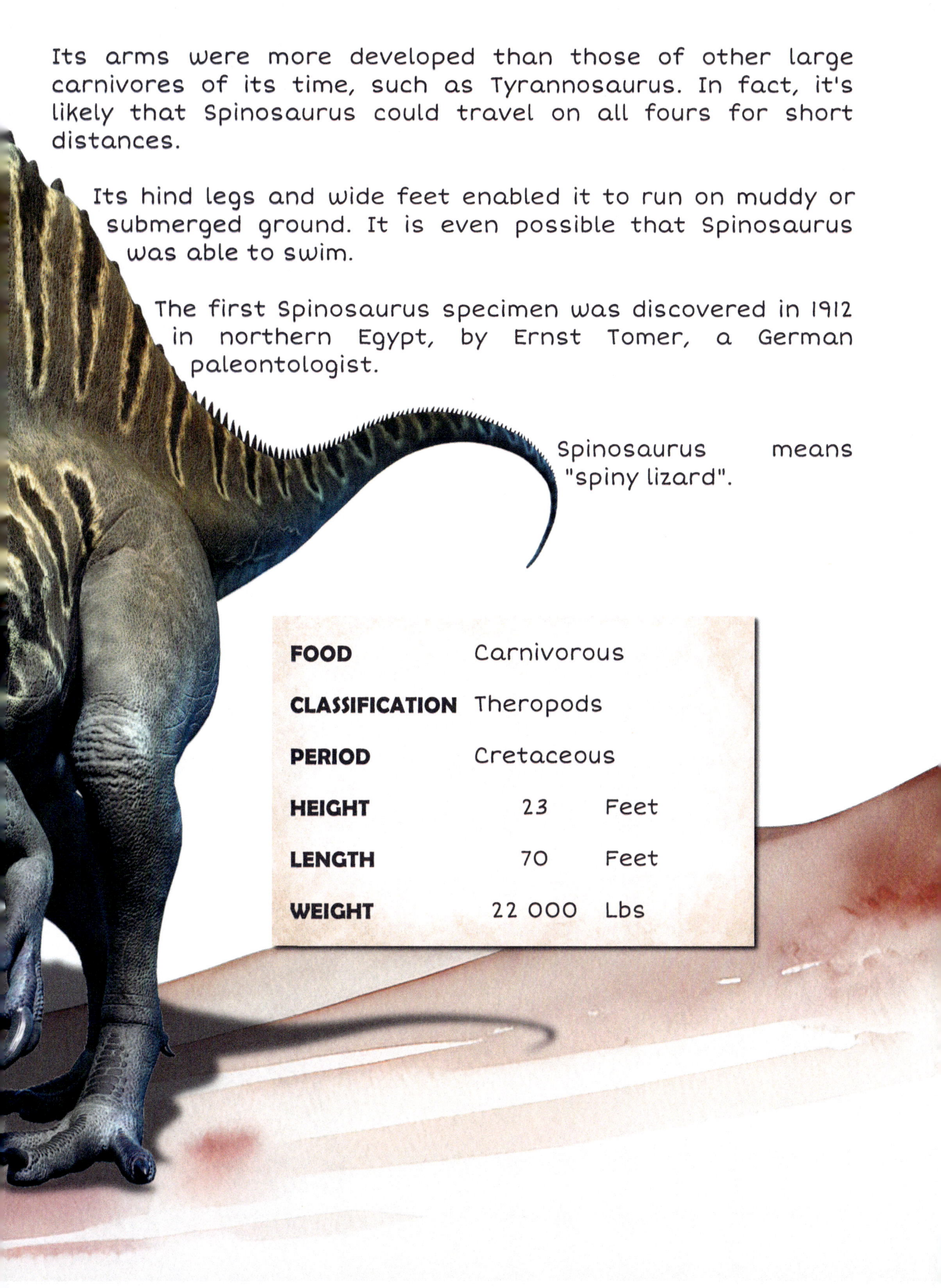

Its arms were more developed than those of other large carnivores of its time, such as Tyrannosaurus. In fact, it's likely that Spinosaurus could travel on all fours for short distances.

Its hind legs and wide feet enabled it to run on muddy or submerged ground. It is even possible that Spinosaurus was able to swim.

The first Spinosaurus specimen was discovered in 1912 in northern Egypt, by Ernst Tomer, a German paleontologist.

Spinosaurus means "spiny lizard".

FOOD	Carnivorous
CLASSIFICATION	Theropods
PERIOD	Cretaceous
HEIGHT	23 Feet
LENGTH	70 Feet
WEIGHT	22 000 Lbs

STEGOSAURUS

Stegosaurus was one of the most easily identifiable dinosaurs.

Bony plates stood out on its back, neck and tail.

These plates certainly had a dual function: to protect the Stegosaurus from attack and avoid a bite to the spine, and to regulate the animal's internal temperature. These plates were in fact criss-crossed by blood vessels. In this way, Stegosaurus could heat up or cool down, depending on whether it was in the sun or shade.

Some paleontologists also believe that these plates, and especially their red color due to blood activity, may have played a role in reproduction, by attracting mates.

Stegosaurus also had four bony spikes at the end of its tail. By whipping its opponent with them, it could inflict serious injuries. These spikes could reach forty inches in length.

The first Stegosaurus fossil was discovered in 1877 in Colorado, North America.

Stegosaurus means "reptile with a roof".

FOOD	Herbivorous
CLASSIFICATION	Thyreophorans
PERIOD	Jurassic
HEIGHT	13 Feet
LENGTH	30 Feet
WEIGHT	6500 Lbs

THERIZINOSAURUS

Therizinosaurus was an enigmatic dinosaur.

First of all, its classification posed many problems for scientists. Because so few fossils had been found, it was initially classified as a turtle! Fifty years after its discovery, it was classified in the theropod family.

Then there's its morphology. Therizinosaurus had very long claws on its upper limbs, measuring up to 28 inches. This anatomical feature is unusual among dinosaurs. These claws could not be used for defense or attack. They were too long, too heavy and too fragile for combat.

Finally, its neck was longer than that of other theropods, and its head was smaller.

It would seem that the Therizinosaurus was truly a dinosaur apart. It could feed on small animals, but its diet was mainly vegetarian. It was therefore one of the few omnivorous dinosaurs known today.

Its claws were probably used to gather plants from marshes and wetlands.

Therizinosaurus was discovered in 1948 in Mongolia.

Therizinosaurus means "reaper reptile".

FOOD	Omnivorous
CLASSIFICATION	Theropods
PERIOD	Cretaceous
HEIGHT	17 Feet
LENGTH	40 Feet
WEIGHT	13 000 Lbs

TRICERATOPS

Triceratops was a herbivorous dinosaur from the late Cretaceous period.

Easily recognizable, its head featured a large bony frill covering the nape of the neck, as well as three horns (two on the forehead and one on the nose). The two long frontal horns were up to forty inches long each.

Triceratops also had a sort of bony beak on the front of its mouth.

Its horns were mainly used to defend itself against large predators, such as the Tyrannosaurus, which lived at the same time and in the same regions.

The bony frill obviously served as protection, like a shield, but paleontologists believe it also served as a thermal regulator.
This organ was highly vascularized, i.e. it had a large network of veins. In this way, Triceratops could regulate its internal temperature by exposing its bony frill to the sun to warm up, or to the shade to cool down.

FOOD	Herbivorous
CLASSIFICATION	Marginocephalians
PERIOD	Cretaceous
HEIGHT	13 Feet
LENGTH	30 Feet
WEIGHT	13 000 Lbs

The first Triceratops fossil was discovered in 1888 in North America.

In 2014, the remains of the largest known Triceratops were discovered in South Dakota. Its skull measured 103 inches long and 79 inches wide. Its frontal horns measured 47 inches. This specimen was nicknamed Big John.

Triceratops means "three-horned head".

TYRANNOSAURUS

Tyrannosaurus, whose full name is "Tyrannosaurus Rex", lived at the end of the Cretaceous period, in North America, China and Mongolia.

This large bipedal carnivore had powerful legs and small arms. Its massive tail served mainly as a balance beam.

Tyrannosaurus was a formidable predator!

Its jaw contained some sixty sharp teeth, each nearly eight inches long. Its teeth were regularly renewed to keep them strong and sharp. Its vision enabled it to detect the slightest movement in its surroundings.

Tyrannosaurus could run at speeds of up to 15 MPH.

Paleontologists believe that Tyrannosaurus' arms gradually atrophied over the course of evolution to compensate for the weight of its head.

The first Tyrannosaurus fossil was discovered in 1902 by Barnum Brown and Henry Fairfield Osborn, in Montana, North America.

The first bones discovered were a femur and a pelvic bone. The bones were so heavy that a sledge had to be built and pulled by horses to transport them to the road.

Tyrannosaurus Rex means "king of the tyrant lizards".

FOOD	Carnivorous
CLASSIFICATION	Theropods
PERIOD	Cretaceous
HEIGHT	20 Feet
LENGTH	43 Feet
WEIGHT	17 500 Lbs

VELAFRONS

Velafrons was an Ornithopod from the Cretaceous period.

This massive herbivore lived in the coastal areas of western North America.

A distinctive feature of this dinosaur was its prominent bony crest at the top of its skull.

We don't know exactly what this crest was used for. It might have been used for defense, but it didn't seem to be totally suited to striking, like the rest of the skull.

It's more likely that it was simply a ceremonial device, a bit like the cock's crest. In this way, the crest could provide information about the dinosaur's sexual nature (male or female) and maturity. Finally, the crest may have helped regulate the Velafrons' temperature.

However, few fossils of this species exist, and it is difficult to establish with certainty the function of this bony outgrowth without knowing its color, precise evolution in terms of growth, and sexual differentiation.

The first fossil was discovered in 2007 in Mexico, North America.

Velafrons means "veil on the forehead".

FOOD	Herbivorous
CLASSIFICATION	Ornithopods
PERIOD	Cretaceous
HEIGHT	10 Feet
LENGTH	26 Feet
WEIGHT	9000 Lbs

VELOCIRAPTOR

Velociraptor was a small bipedal carnivore that lived at the end of the Cretaceous period.

Much depicted in dinosaur movies, the Velociraptor was actually smaller than most people think.

Its morphology enabled it to reach a running speed of 38 MPH.

Its jaw possessed 80 sharp teeth.

Analysis of its skull shows that the volume of its brain was relatively large compared with its size, suggesting that this dinosaur had a higher intelligence than other predators of its time.

Velociraptor had a six-inch curved, retractable claw on the inner toe of its hind limbs. This claw enabled it to tear or disembowel its prey.

In 1971, an incredible fossil was discovered in Mongolia. It was the fossil of a Velociraptor and a Protoceratops. The two dinosaurs were certainly in battle when a sand dune buried them. One of the Velociraptor's claws was stuck in the neck of the Protoceratops.

The first Velociraptor fossil was discovered in 1922 in Mongolia's Gobi Desert.

Velociraptor means "swift thief".

FOOD	Carnivorous
CLASSIFICATION	Theropods
PERIOD	Cretaceous
HEIGHT	4 Feet
LENGTH	6.5 Feet
WEIGHT	45 Lbs

FLYING REPTILES

Flying reptiles weren't dinosaurs, but they lived alongside them every day.

This large reptile family, called Pterosaurs, is divided into two groups:
- The Pterodactyloidea, which had a very short tail and a wing supported by a single finger.
- The more archaic Rhamphorhynchidea, with longer tails and shorter wings.

ANHANGUERA

Anhanguera was a flying reptile that lived in what is now South America, but also in Europe.

Its immense wings had a fifteen-foot wingspan. The wingspan is the total width of a bird when its wings are fully extended. In other words, it's the distance between the two wingtips in the extended position.

Anhanguera's wings, like those of other Pterosaurs of the same family, were made of a membrane of skin stretched between the fingers. A single finger (the fourth) supported the outer half of the wing, from its middle to its tip.

Its long, splayed jaw contained long, sharp teeth.

Anhanguera lived in coastal areas and large bodies of water (large lakes, for example).

It ate mainly fish, which it caught on the surface of the water with its powerful jaws. It is likely that the Anhanguera also fed on carrion (i.e. animal corpses) and insects. It's worth noting that, at the time, there were some very large insects. The giant dragonfly, Meganeura, for example, had a wingspan of over twelve inches. An excellent meal for Anhanguera!

Given its slender hind legs, Anhanguera must have spent most of its time flying.

The first fossil was discovered in 1985 in Brazil.

Anhanguera means "old devil".

FOOD	Piscivorous
CLASSIFICATION	Pterodactyloidea
PERIOD	Cretaceous
WINGSPAN	15 Feet
LENGTH	5 Feet
WEIGHT	275 Lbs

DIMORPHODON

Dimorphodon lived in the Jurassic period.

It is one of the oldest Pterosaurs known today.

Analysis of its skeleton reveals that the size of its wings did not allow Dimorphodon to fly long distances. It is likely that it even moved mostly on the ground, like a quadruped, and climbed trees to rest out of reach of predators.

For a long time, scientists believed that Dimorphodon fed on fish. But such a diet would have required this little reptile to be adept at flying, and this was not the case. In reality, Dimorphodon fed on insects, small reptiles and mammals.

The first Dimorphodon fossils were discovered in England in 1828, by Mary Anning, a fossil collector.

Dimorphodon means "two forms of teeth".

Indeed, Dimorphodon had two types of teeth: Long, pointed teeth on the front of its jaws, and short, flat teeth on the back. This feature is rare in reptiles, whether terrestrial, flying or aquatic.

FOOD	Carnivorous
CLASSIFICATION	Rhamphorhynchoidea
PERIOD	Jurassic
WINGSPAN	4.5 Feet
LENGTH	3 Feet
WEIGHT	5 Lbs

PTERODACTYL

Pterodactyl was a flying reptile of modest size.

It was the first flying reptile to be discovered and identified.

Pterodactyl ate mainly fish and other small vertebrates.
It had 90 teeth in its jaws.
A crest adorned the top of its skull. This appendage consisted mainly of soft tissue (flesh, skin), but also had a bony base.

Like all flying reptiles, the Pterodactyl was oviparous. It laid eggs in nests built high up on cliffs, for example.

The first Pterodactyl fossils were discovered in Germany, in Bavaria to be precise. At the time of discovery, the wing membrane had obviously disappeared. The skeleton therefore revealed a very long finger (the fourth) at wing level. This greatly disturbed scientists.

In 1784, the Italian scientist Cosimo Alessandro Colline identified it as an aquatic reptile.

In 1800, French scientist Jean Hermann hypothesized that the reptile's fourth finger supported a membrane wing.

In 1809, Georges Cuvier, a French paleontologist, classified it for the first time in the flying reptile family.

Pterodactyl means "winged finger".

FOOD	Piscivorous
CLASSIFICATION	Pterodactyloidea
PERIOD	Jurassic
WINGSPAN	3.2 Feet
LENGTH	2 Feet
WEIGHT	4.5 Lbs

QUETZALCOATLUS

Quetzalcoatlus was a huge Pterosaur.

Its wingspan was thirty-three feet, and its total length in flight was twenty-six feet (from the tip of its beak to the tip of its hind legs, which were horizontal during flight). On the ground, it was twenty feet high.

Its body was covered with dense hairs called pycnofibre. In reality, these fine, supple filaments were a structure between hair and feather.
In fact, most pterosaurs were covered in them.

Quetzalcoatlus had a huge beak, up to five feet long.

Quetzalcoatlus most likely fed on fish caught in large freshwater lakes, as well as on vertebrates (amphibians, mammals, etc.).

Despite its size, the Quetzalcoatlus could take off from the ground. At least, that's what some paleontologists think. In order to take off, the Quetzalcoatlus made a jump, opening its wings and providing the necessary impetus for flight.

The first Quetzalcoatlus fossil was discovered in 1971 in Texas (USA).

The name Quetzalcoatlus comes from "Quetzalcóatl", a god of the Aztec, Mayan and Toltec civilizations. He was also known as the "feathered serpent".

FOOD	Piscivorous
CLASSIFICATION	Pterodactyloidea
PERIOD	Cretaceous
WINGSPAN	32 Feet
LENGTH	26 Feet
WEIGHT	550 Lbs

THALASSODROMEUS

Thalassodromeus lived in the regions of present-day Brazil.

Its beak had no teeth, but its edges were very sharp.

Its skull was easily recognizable, with a large bony crest. It could be heard from the tip of its beak to the back of its skull. Despite its size, it was light.

Scientists still wonder about the precise function of this crest.

It is likely that it had several functions. Firstly, it may have helped regulate the Thalassodromeus's temperature. Secondly, it was almost certainly a signal of sexual maturity, growing larger as Thalassodromeus aged.

Paleontologists don't know exactly how Thalassodromeus fed. They first thought it fed on fish, catching them on the surface of the water in mid-flight, but the size and shape of the jaw don't seem compatible.

The most likely hypothesis is that Thalassodromeus fed on the ground, capturing insects and even large prey such as reptiles, amphibians and mammals.

Thalassodromeus was discovered in 1983 in Brazil.

Thalassodromeus means "sea runner".

FOOD	Piscivorous
CLASSIFICATION	Pterodactyloidea
PERIOD	Cretaceous
WINGSPAN	15 Feet
LENGTH	5 Feet
WEIGHT	25 Lbs

MARINE REPTILES

Like flying reptiles, marine reptiles are not dinosaurs, but they lived at the same time.

Their classification is complex, given the multiple differences between species.

While dinosaurs ruled the earth, these fearsome predators reigned supreme over the oceans.

ELASMOSAURUS

Elasmosaurus was a gigantic marine reptile.

It could measure up to forty-six feet in length. Its neck comprised 76 vertebrae and was more than half its size.

To move about on the seabed, Elasmosaurus used its four flipper-like limbs. However, its morphology suggests that it could not evolve in water too deep.

It should also be noted that Elasmosaurus was a reptile, and therefore breathed air. It was not a fish. It therefore had to seek air at the water's surface on a regular basis, like crocodiles (which are reptiles) or dolphins (which are mammals).

Despite its size, Elasmosaurus most certainly fed on modest-sized fish, as well as other marine animals, such as primitive cephalopods.

The first fossil was discovered in 1867 in Kansas, USA.

A year later, Edward Drinker Cope, an American paleontologist, received the bones and began to study them. However, he made a mistake when reconstructing the skeleton. He placed the skull at the end of the tail, not at the end of the neck. This left Elasmosaurus with a small neck and a very long tail. It was Othniel Charles Marsh who pointed out the error to his colleague.

Elasmosaurus means "ribbon reptile".

FOOD	Piscivorous
CLASSIFICATION	Plesiosauroidea
PERIOD	Jurassic - Cretaceous
HEIGHT	10 Feet
LENGTH	46 Feet
WEIGHT	4500 Lbs

EURHINOSAURUS

Eurhinosaurus more or less resembled a dolphin (a mammal) or a swordfish (a fish).

Yet Eurhinosaurus was indeed a reptile.

It was a fast swimmer, certainly reaching speeds of at least 40 MPH. It evolved in fairly deep waters around Europe.

One of the special features of Eurhinosaurus was its upper jaw, which was twice as long as its lower jaw. This rostrum (a sort of bony extension of the nose) could measure up to five feet, and had outward-facing teeth.

Eurhinosaurus hunted fish by striking them with its rostrum, causing serious injuries due to the violence of the impact. In addition, the teeth positioned on the side tore prey apart.

Like most Ichthyosaurs, Eurhinosaurus had relatively large eyes. What's more, as the analysis of fossilized skulls proves, these reptiles had excellent hearing. They detected their prey by underwater vibrations and hunted by sight.

The first Eurhinosaurus fossil was discovered in Germany in 1909.

Eurhinosaurus means "reptile with a big nose".

FOOD	Piscivorous
CLASSIFICATION	Ichtyosaurs
PERIOD	Jurassic
HEIGHT	6 Feet
LENGTH	23 Feet
WEIGHT	4400 Lbs

LIOPLEURODON

Liopleurodon was a Jurassic marine reptile.

It lived in the regions of present-day Europe. During the Jurassic, much of Western Europe was covered by water.

Like all Pliosaurs, Liopleurodon had a long, flattened head, rather like that of a crocodile. It had a short neck and a massive body. Finally, it had four fins and a tail.

Its general morphology and the shape of its fins show that Liopleurodon was capable of sudden acceleration. It certainly hunted on the prowl. As soon as a prey item came within its reach, it sprang up and captured it.

Liopleurodon fed on fish, squid and other aquatic reptiles.

The first fossils were discovered around 1840. It was Henri Charles Sauvage, a French paleontologist, who gave it the name Liopleurodon in 1873.

In 1999, a television program presented the Liopleurodon as an immense reptile over 80 feet long and weighing 33,000 pounds. Recent scientific studies show that these dimensions were greatly exaggerated, and that the Liopleurodon measured an average of 23 feet in adulthood.

Liopleurodon means "smooth-faced teeth".

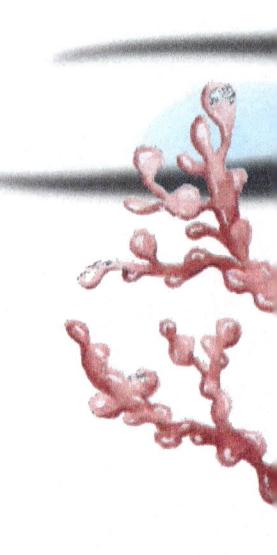

FOOD	Piscivorous
CLASSIFICATION	Pliosauridea
PERIOD	Jurassic
HEIGHT	5 Feet
LENGTH	23 Feet
WEIGHT	4000 Lbs

NOTHOSAURUS

Nothosaurus was both a marine and a terrestrial reptile.

It had no fins, but rather webbed feet. It could therefore evolve on land, but also in an aquatic environment.

FOOD	Piscivorous
CLASSIFICATION	Nothosauridae
PERIOD	Triassic
HEIGHT	3 Feet
LENGTH	10 Feet
WEIGHT	330 Lbs

Its legs alone were insufficient for underwater travel, and Nothosaurus relied mainly on its tail for propulsion.

Its dentition suggests that it fed mainly on aquatic species. Indeed, its long, fine, pointed teeth are perfectly suited to gripping fish.

Its mode of reproduction was that of a terrestrial reptile. It laid eggs and buried them in the ground, most certainly on sandy beaches.
However, given the morphology of Nothosaurus, mating must have taken place in the water.

Nothosaurus lived along the coasts of Europe, North Africa and Asia.

Some paleontologists believe that reptiles like Nothosaurus may have evolved into reptiles of the Plesiosaurus family.

The first fossil was discovered in 1834 in Germany.

Nothosaurus means "mixed lizard".

TYLOSAURUS

Tylosaurus was a reptile of the Mosasauridae family. Visually, the reptiles of this family somewhat resembled the reptiles of the Pliosaur family. However, they are in fact two distinct families.

Generally speaking, reptiles of the Mosasauridae family had lizard-like heads and very long tails. Varanids, for example, are descendants of Mosasauridae.

Tylosaurus was a very large marine predator. Up to forty-six feet long, it scoured the oceans around North America, as well as in Europe, Africa and South America.

Tylosaurus had an oval-shaped skull, with a long, robust, bony snout. It probably charged at its prey and struck them full force with its snout.

It was a ferocious predator, hunting in shallow waters. It preyed on fish and turtles, as well as birds and land animals venturing into the water. In 1918, a Tylosaurus fossil was discovered with the remains of a young Plesiosaurus in its stomach.

The first fossils were discovered in 1868 in Kansas (USA).

Tylosaurus means "lizard with a protuberance", referring to the shape of its head.

FOOD	Piscivorous
CLASSIFICATION	Mosasauridae
PERIOD	Cretaceous
HEIGHT	7 Feet
LENGTH	46 Feet
WEIGHT	22 000 Lbs

EXTINCTION

After 190 million years of reign, the dinosaurs disappeared.
This extinction, which occurred at the end of the Cretaceous period, has long puzzled scientists, and is still the subject of much debate.
What is certain is that the dinosaurs became extinct 66 million years ago, along with a large proportion of other plant and animal species.

THE END OF THE DINOSAURS

66 million years ago, around 75% of the Earth's flora and fauna disappeared.

But how do we know when this event took place?

Once again, it's thanks to fossils. As we saw at the start of this book, paleontologists study geological layers to date fossils.

They use various techniques, such as radiometry, to date the age of a rock.

The layer corresponding to the Cretaceous period is the last to contain dinosaur fossils.

The next layer, corresponding to the Paleocene period, contains none. The Paleocene is a period of the Cenozoic era, following on from the Cretaceous.

Which brings us to the most important question of all: Why did the dinosaurs disappear?

Today, most scientists believe that the extinction of the dinosaurs was due to several major events.

At the end of the Cretaceous, the climate cooled. The cause is uncertain, but it's likely that continental movements were partly responsible.

This period was also marked by a fall in ocean levels, which certainly contributed to the drop in temperatures.

These events had an impact on both fauna (animals) and flora (plants). Some species were able to adapt, others not. What is certain is that many living species were weakened during this period.

Also at the end of the Cretaceous, volcanic activity on Earth was very high. In the Indian region, huge volcanoes spewed out lava in phenomenal quantities.

These eruptions released large quantities of dust and gas, helping to lower temperatures and modify the atmosphere.

Finally, a few decades ago, scientists discovered a thin layer of black clay between the Cretaceous and Paleocene geological layers in several places on Earth. This layer contains high levels of Iridium, a metal that is very rare on Earth, but abundant in certain meteorites.

Scientists therefore hypothesized that a gigantic asteroid would have crashed into Earth during this period.

In the 90s, studies led to the discovery of the Chicxulub crater in Mexico's Yucatan region. This is a crater carved out by the impact of an asteroid, which would have fallen to Earth 66 million years ago. The crater measures 180 kilometers in diameter (112 miles), and 20 kilometers deep (12.5 miles).

Scientists estimate that the asteroid must have been several tens of kilometers in diameter.

On impact, the amount of energy released was immense. Several million nuclear bombs would have to be detonated to achieve the same result.

The impact had immediate and catastrophic consequences: astronomical quantities of dust, ash and gas were thrown into the atmosphere. The shockwave triggered a gigantic tsunami that ravaged coastal regions and a massive earthquake on a planetary scale.

These immediate consequences certainly destroyed a large part of the flora and fauna in just a few hours.

But the long-term consequences were equally catastrophic. The immense cloud of particles (dust, ash, etc.) gradually spread and enveloped the entire Earth, plunging it into darkness for several years.

Deprived of sunlight, the Earth suddenly cooled. Plants, for which light is indispensable, quickly withered away. Herbivores, which feed on plants, also gradually disappeared for lack of food. Finally, the lack of food affected carnivores, who could no longer find enough prey to feed on.

So the dinosaurs disappeared... But other animals, able to adapt to these extreme conditions, managed to survive. These included small mammals, reptiles and insects.

But are we really sure that the dinosaurs all disappeared?

THE LEGACY OF THE DINOSAURS

At the start of this book, we saw that dinosaurs were divided into two major groups, the Saurischians and the Ornithischians.

We'll now turn our attention to the Saurischians, and more specifically to the Theropod group.

The Theropods were carnivorous dinosaurs, like the Tyrannosaurus for example.

But what if I told you that theropods still exist?

Because birds are Theropods! To be precise, birds belong to the Aves family. And Aves are theropods.

It's not all that surprising. As we've seen, some dinosaurs, particularly theropods, had feathers, like Archaeopteryx for example.

Over the millennia, smaller theropods continued to evolve. Little by little, the morphology of their bodies, and above all their upper limbs (i.e. arms), adapted to flight.

And these little dinosaurs managed to survive the cataclysm at the end of the Cretaceous.

It's likely that their small size contributed to their survival. Their diet of insects, small animals and even seeds enabled them to feed despite the catastrophic events of 66 million years ago.

By 1868, British biologist Thomas Huxley had already demonstrated the similarities between theropods and ostriches. The many scientific discoveries of the last century have proved him right.

The next time you look at a bird in your garden, remember that Tyrannosaurus was one of its ancient cousins.

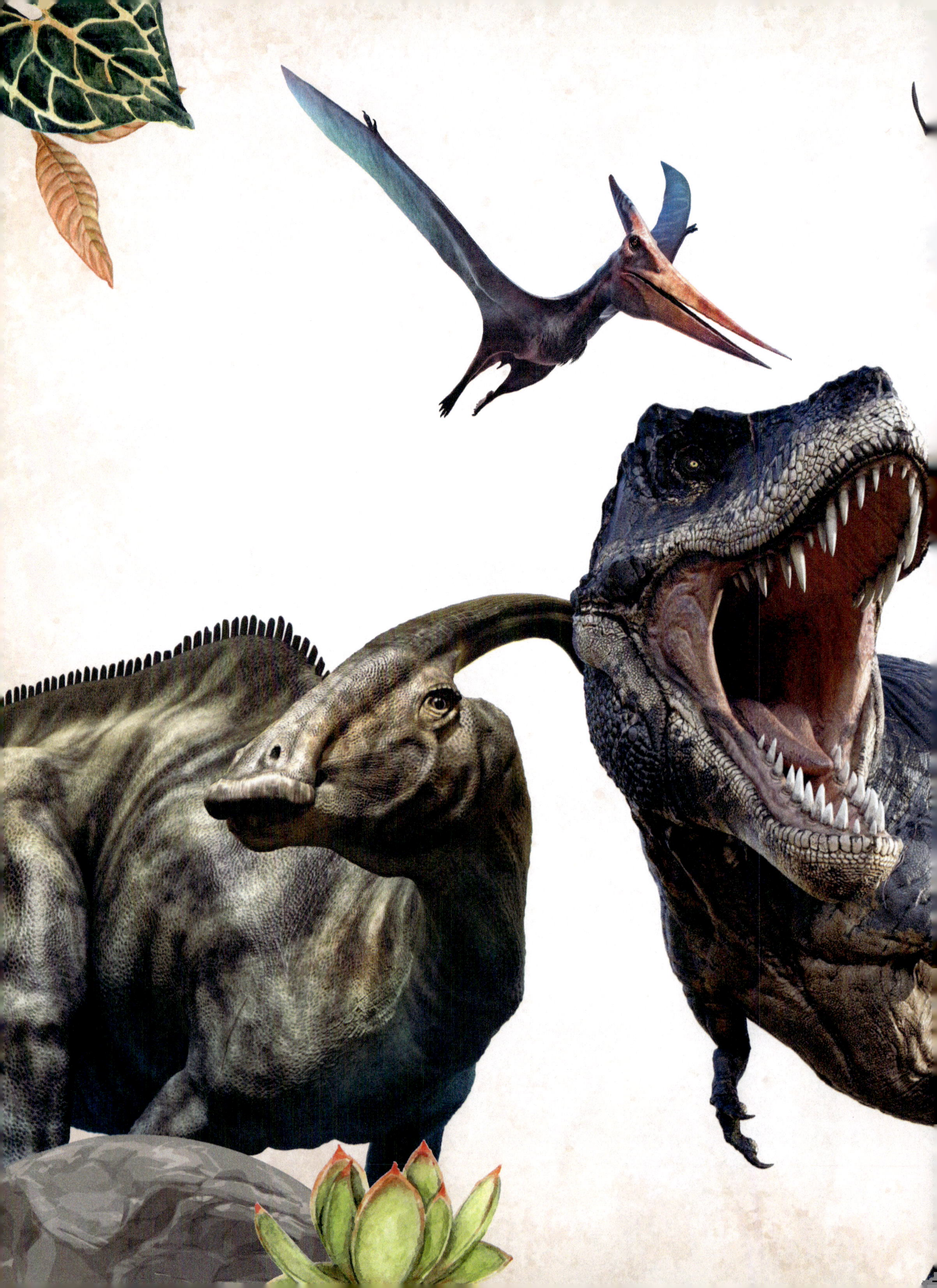

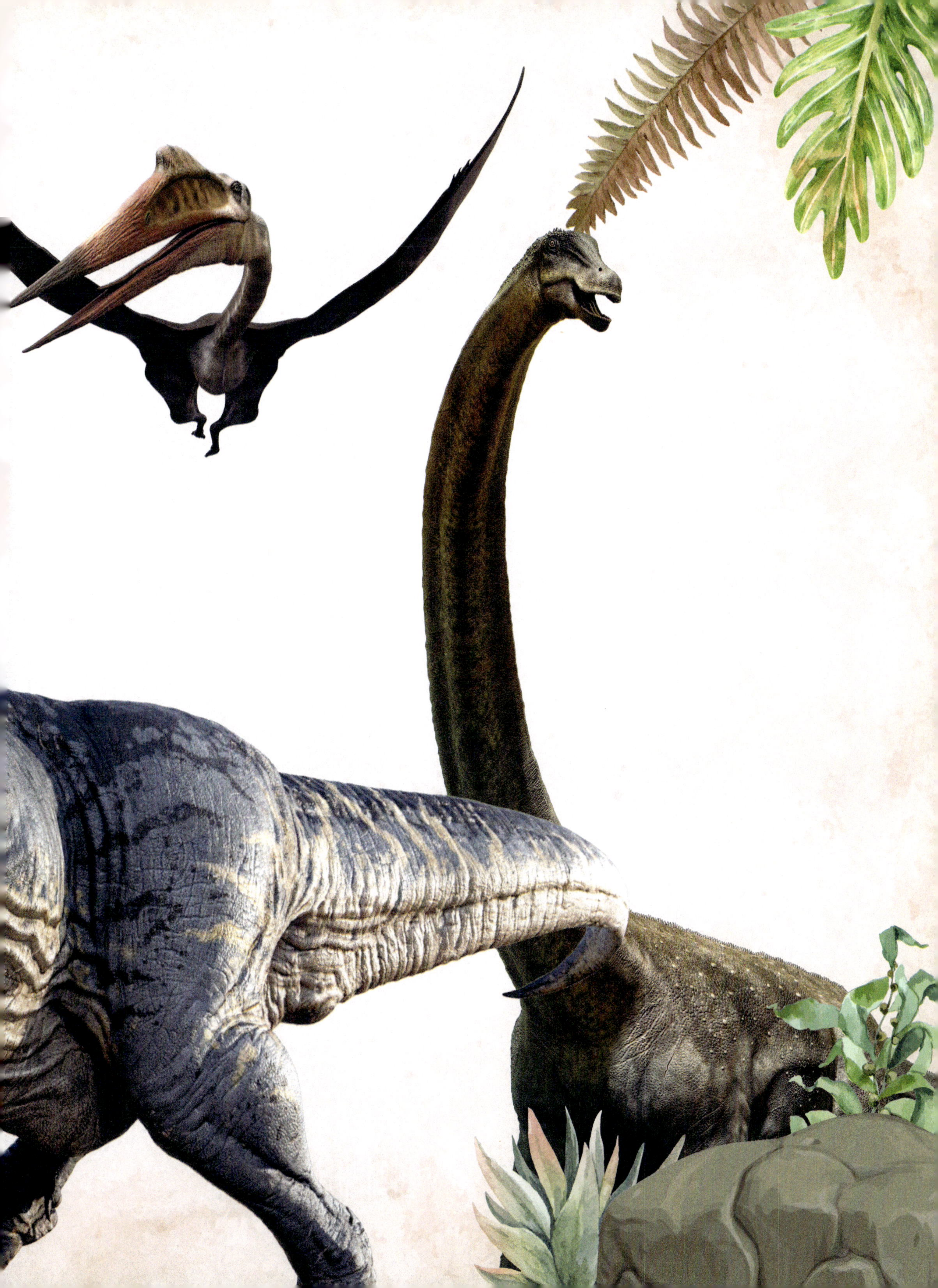

Printed in Great Britain
by Amazon